KNIGHT

An Art Coloring Book

By

Christopher Finn

Published by the Author

2010

www.finncoloringbooks.com

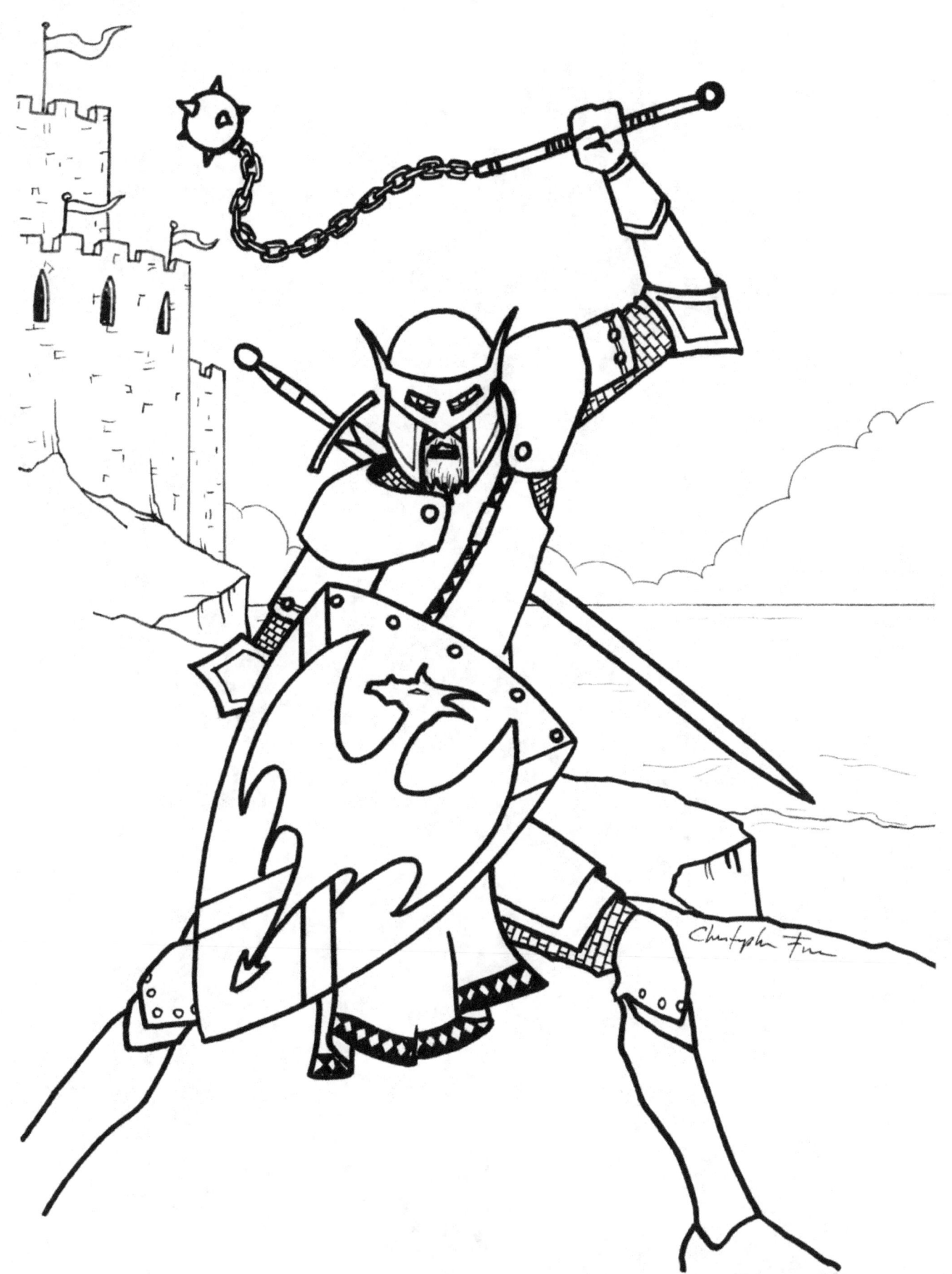

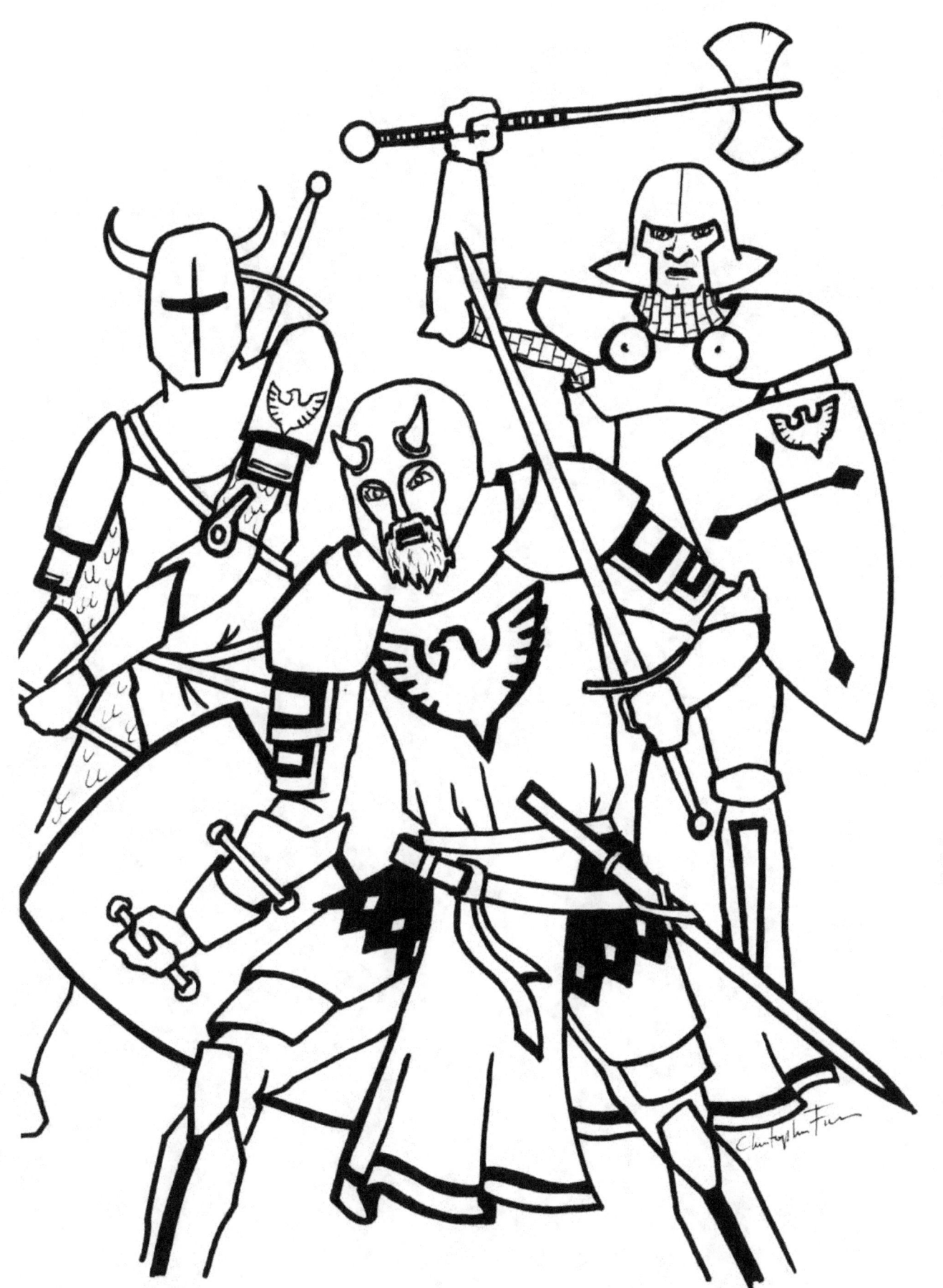

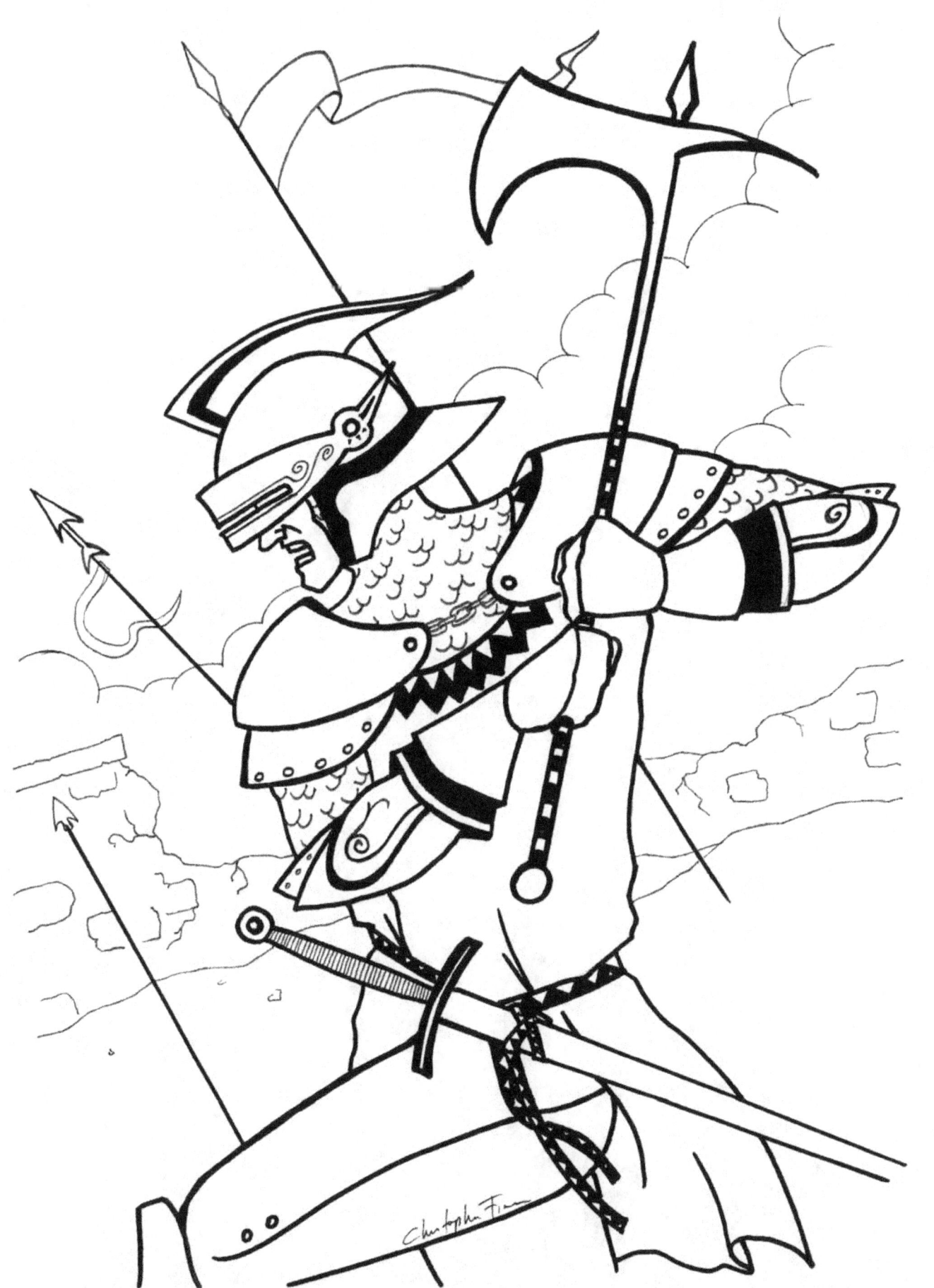

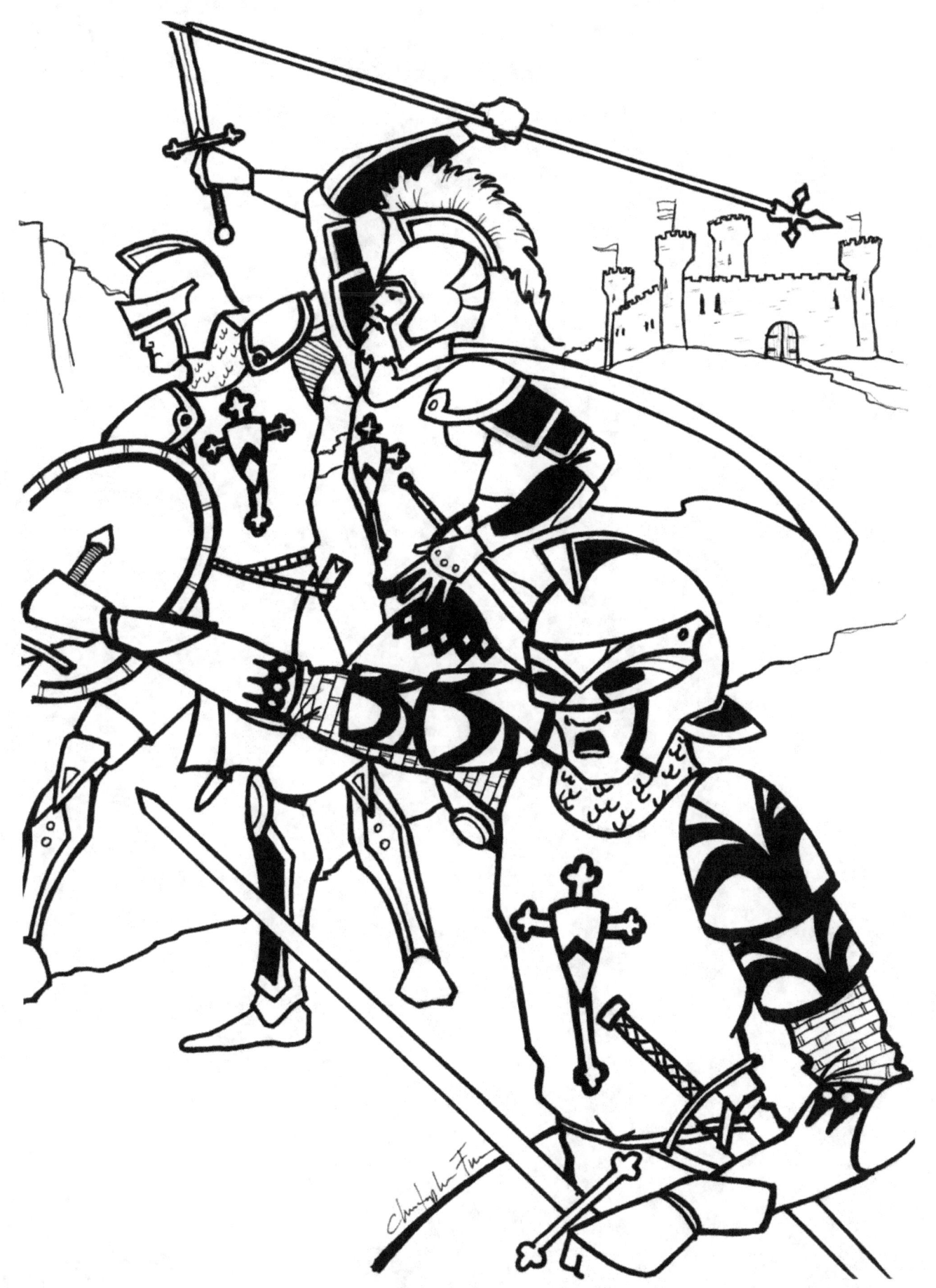

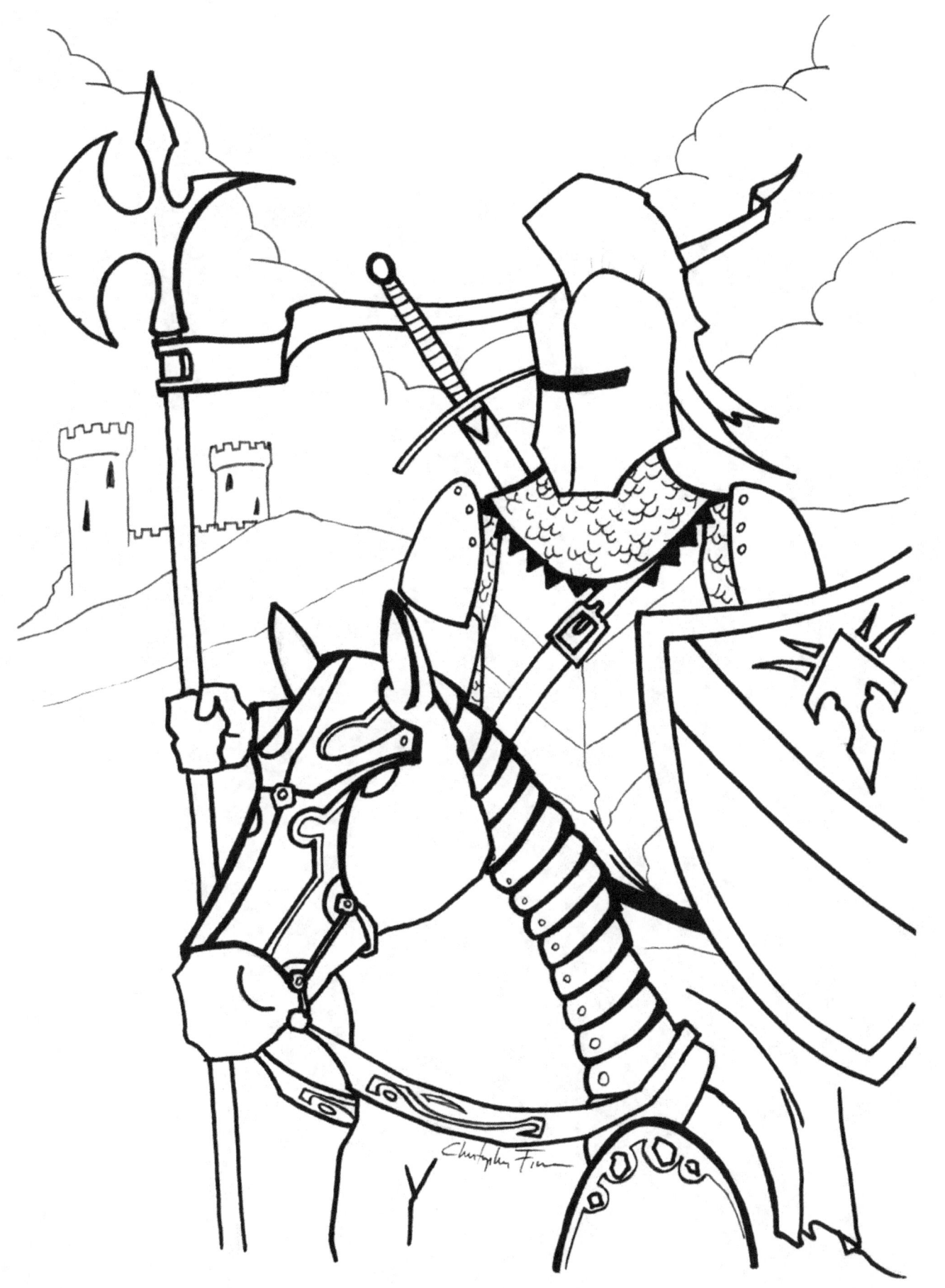

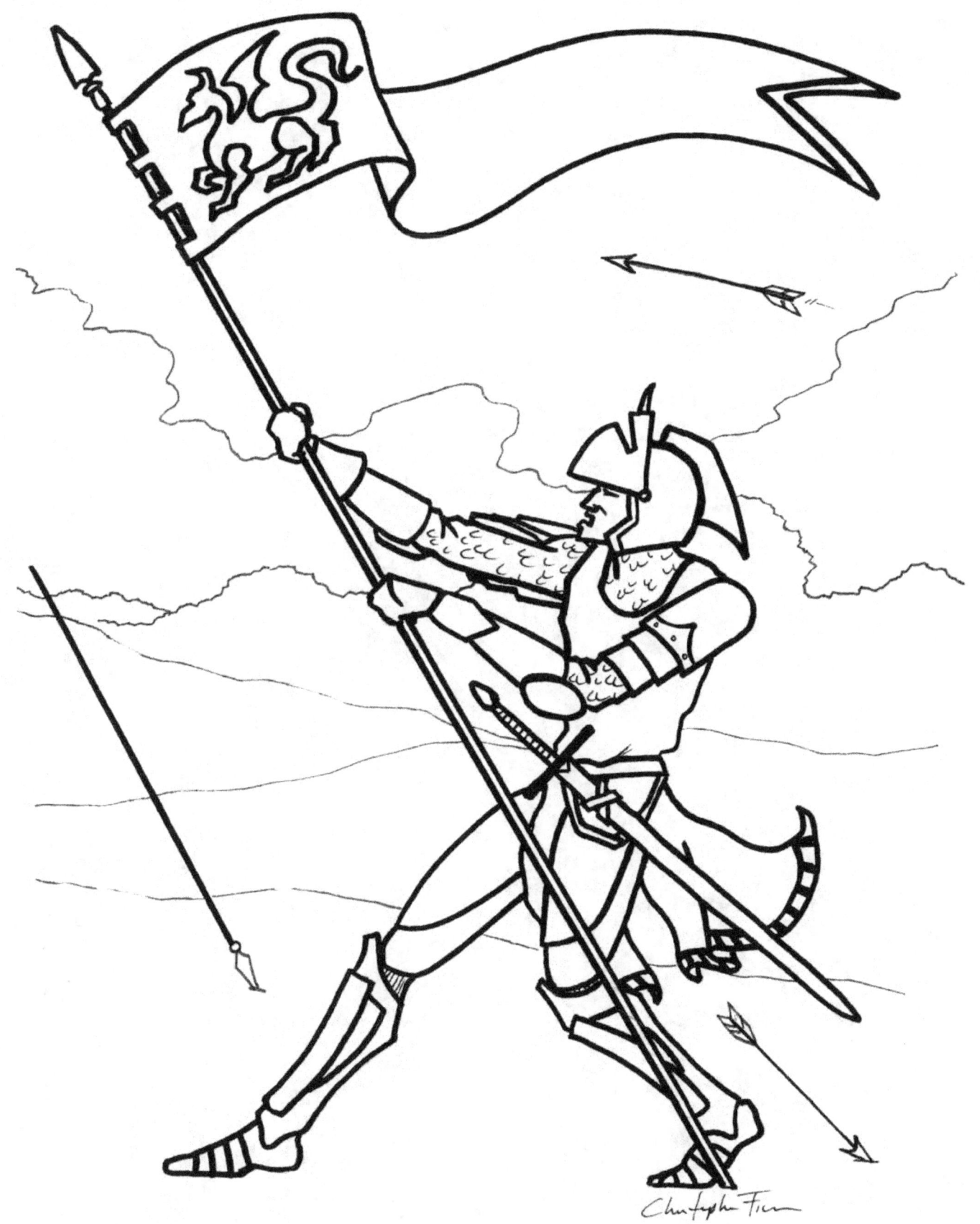

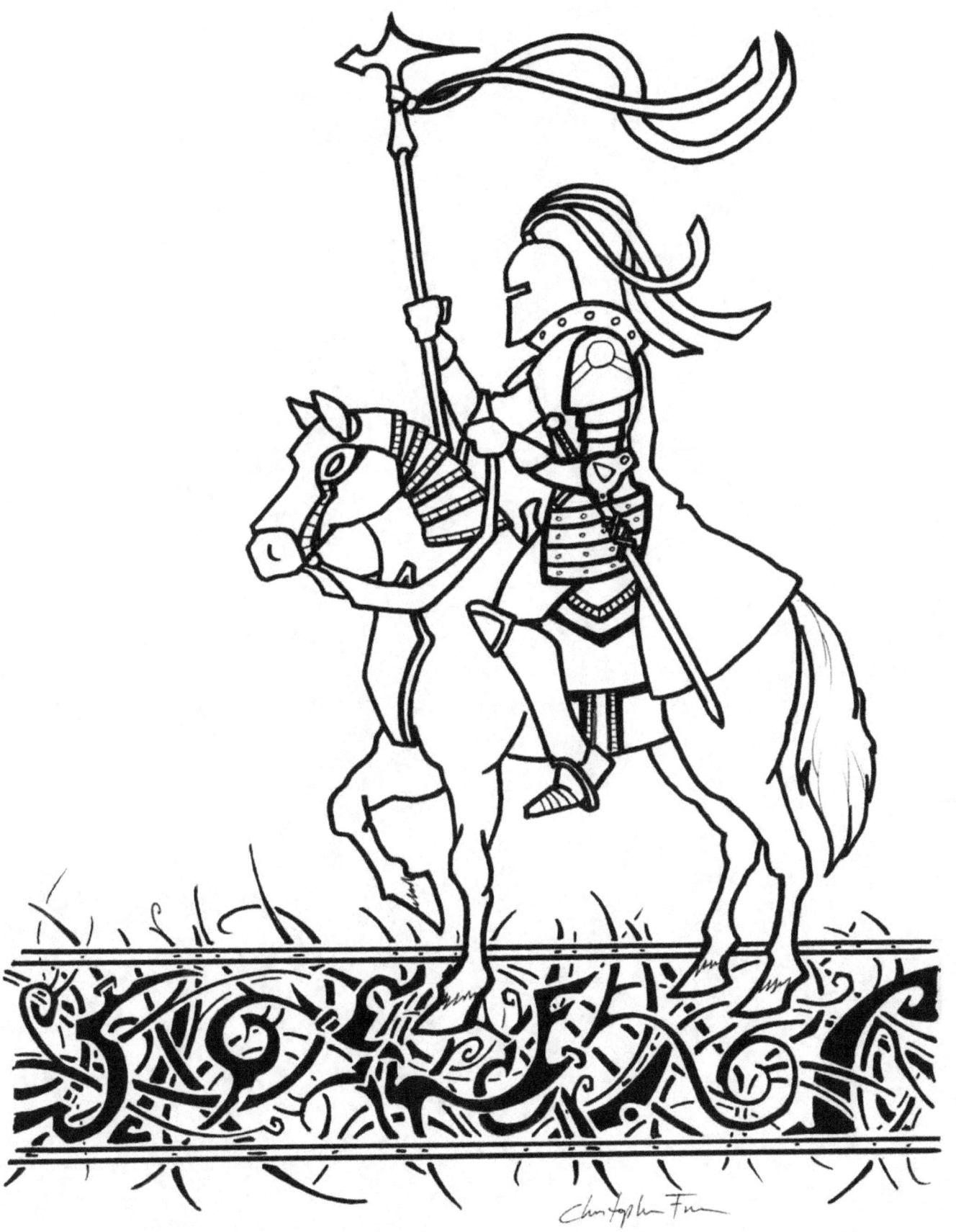

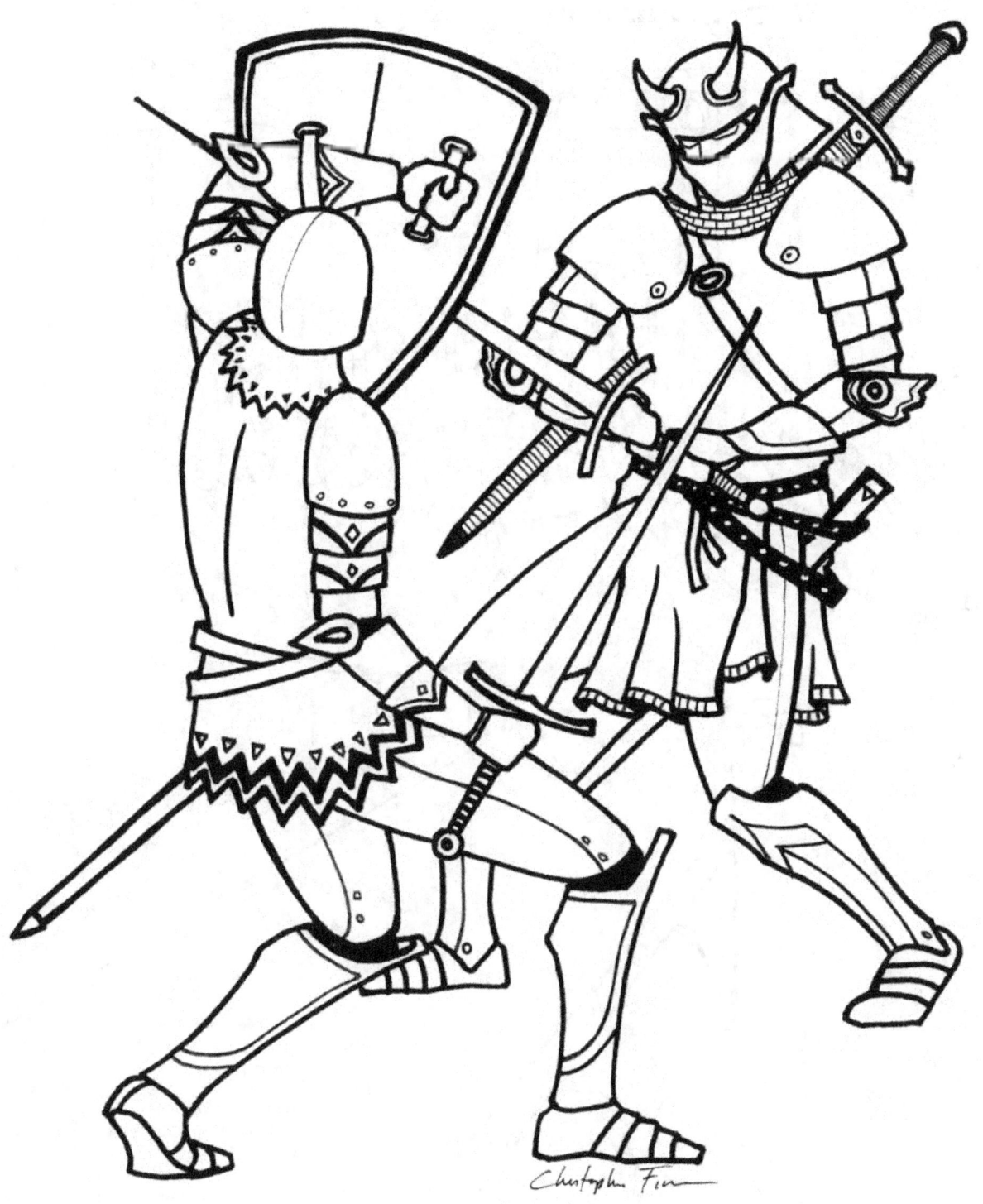

Christopher F_____

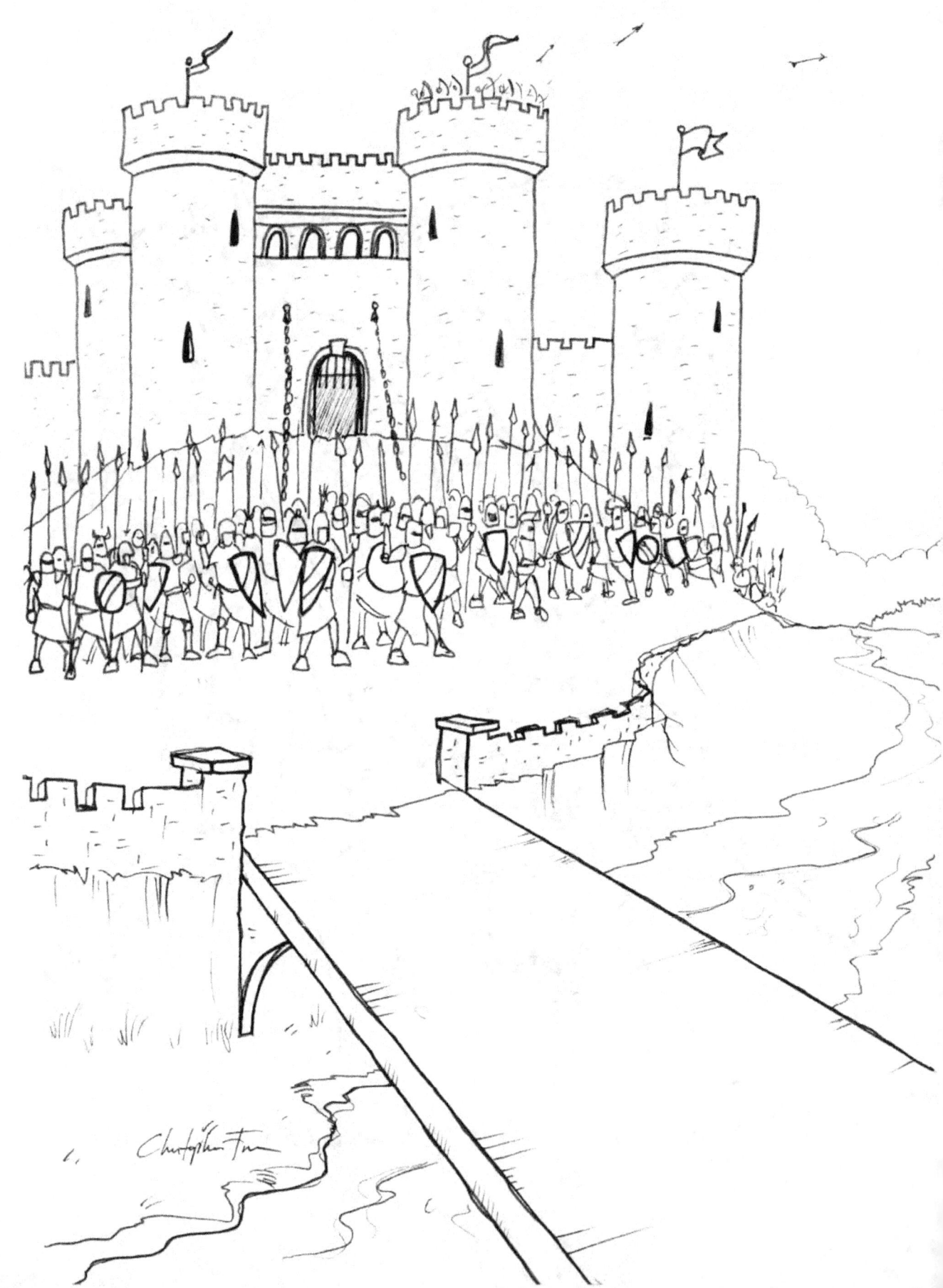

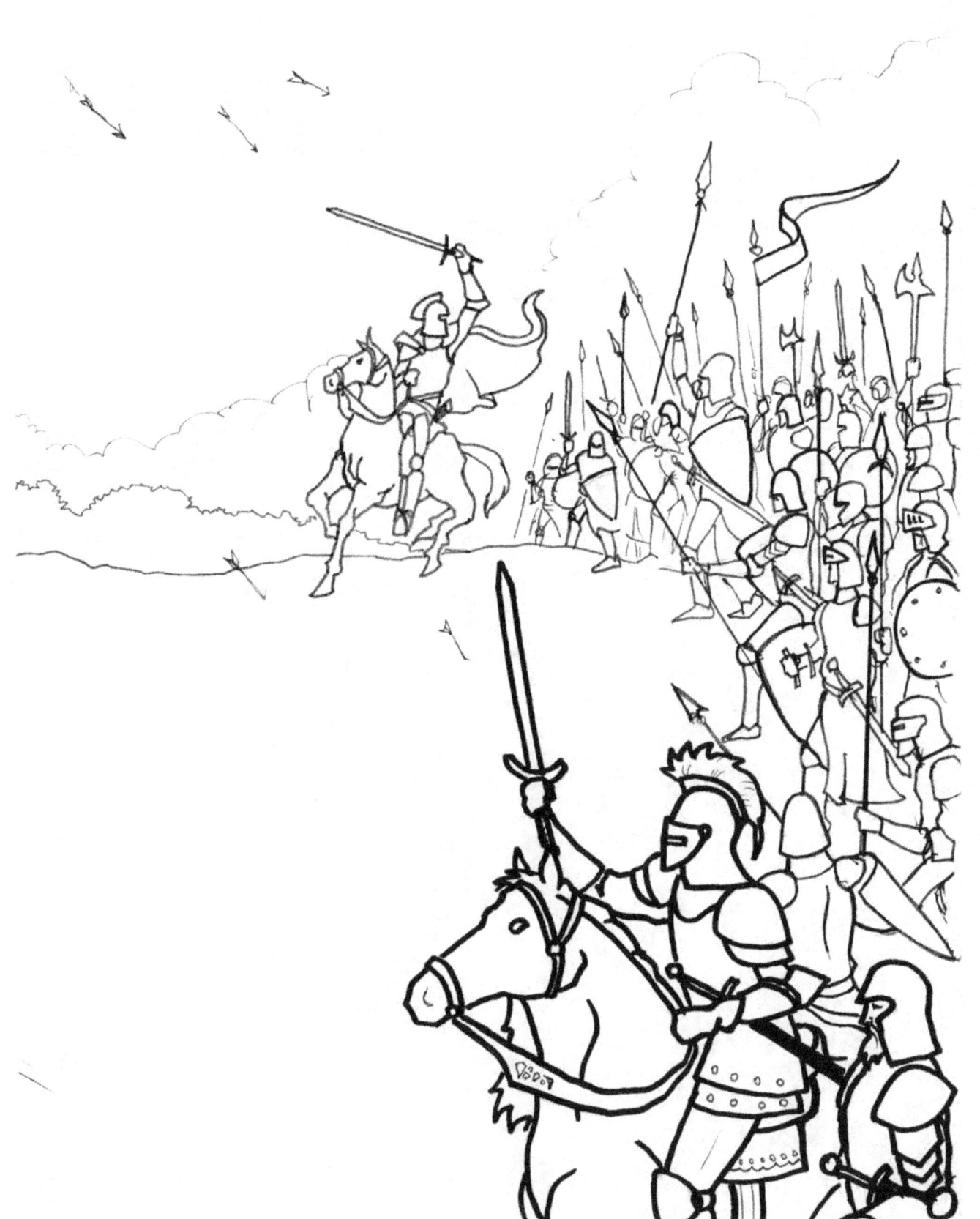

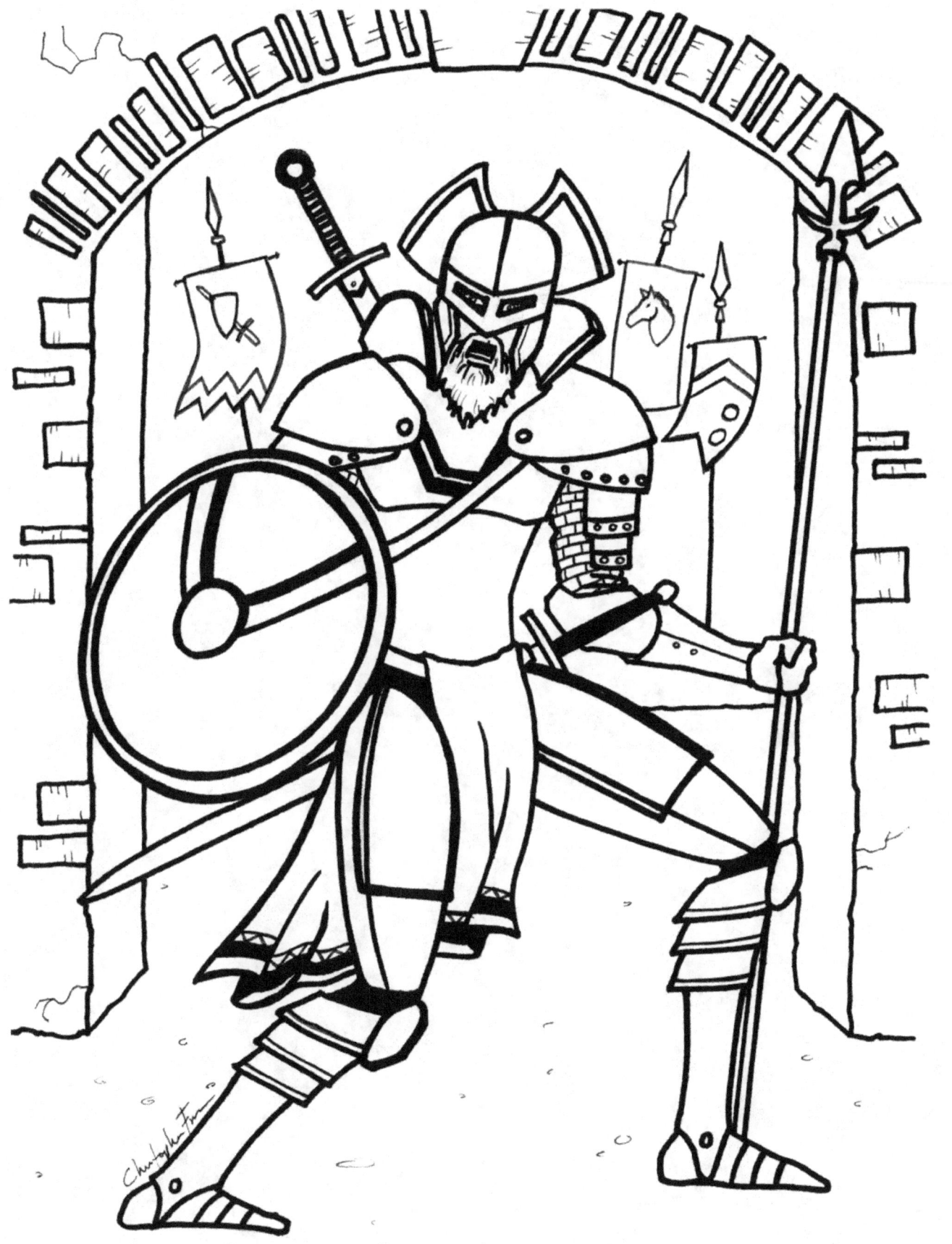

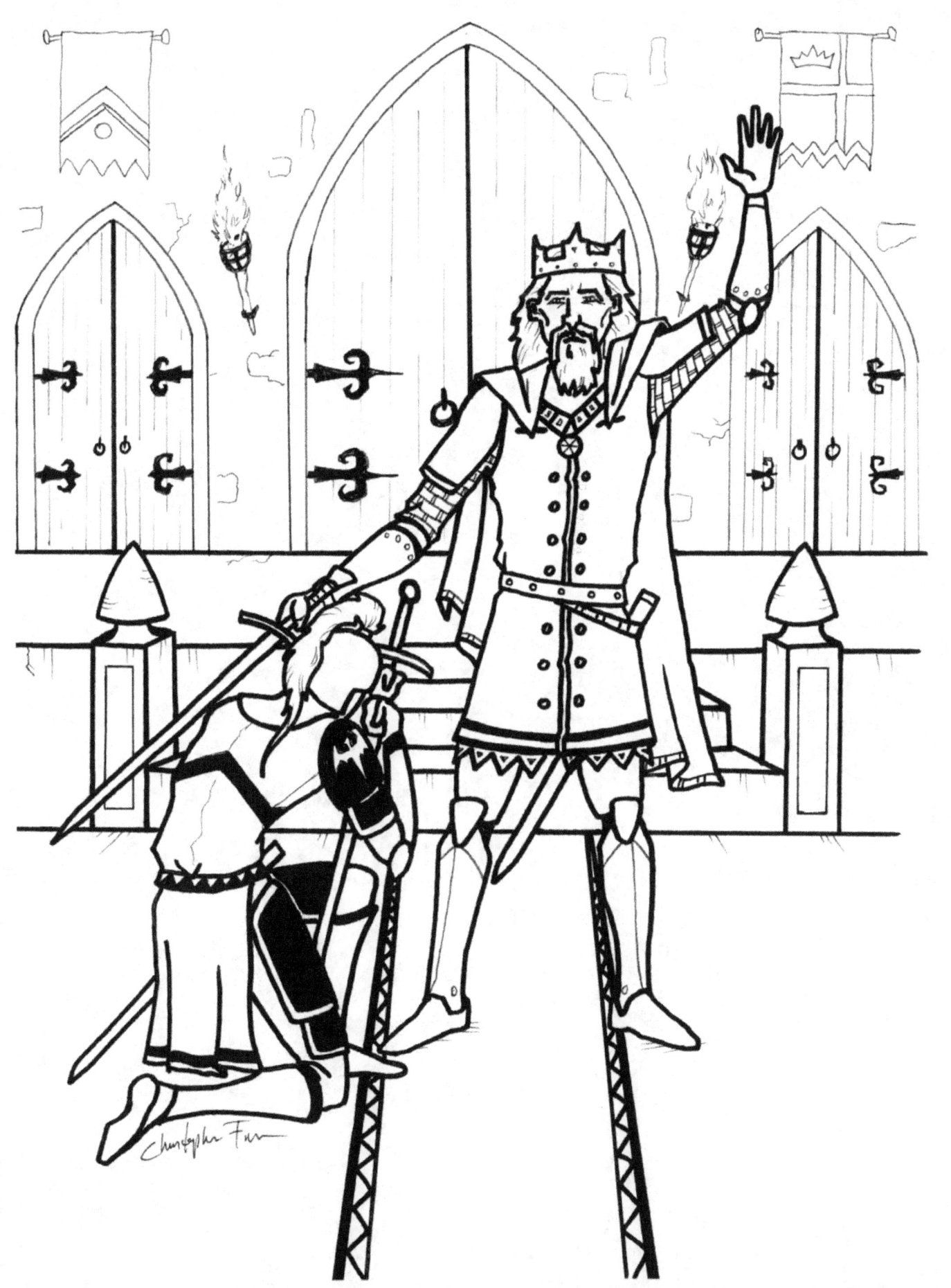

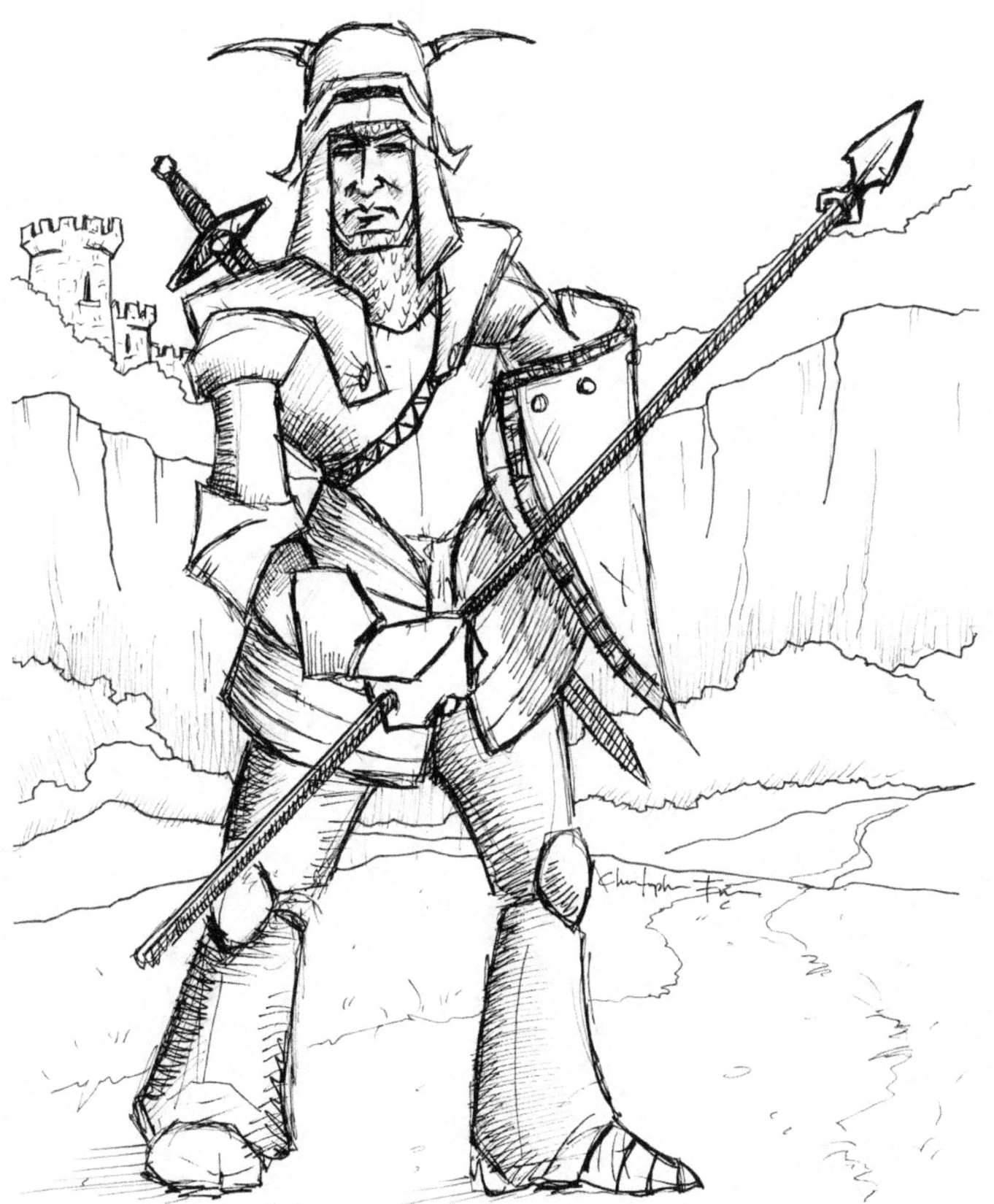

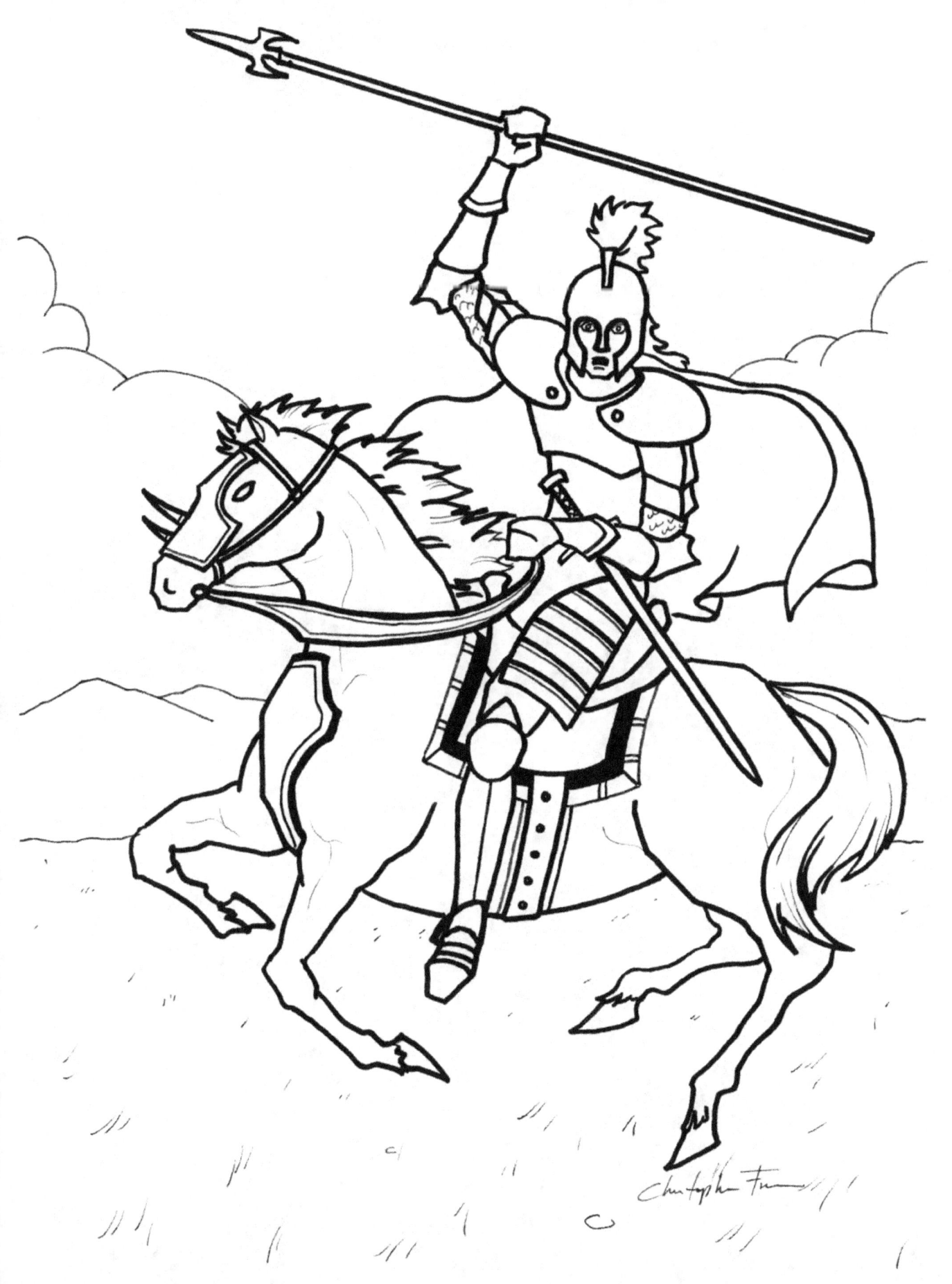

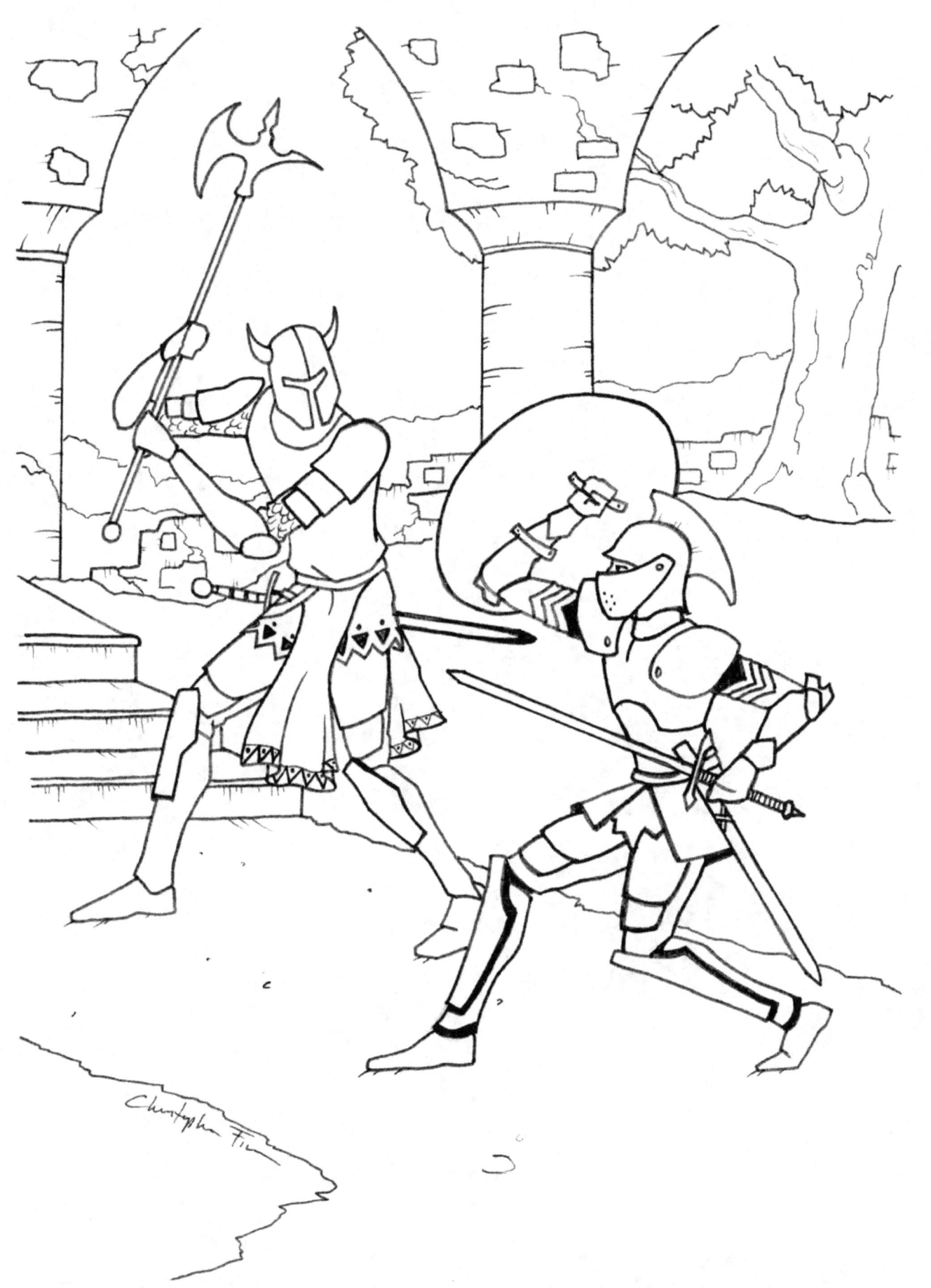

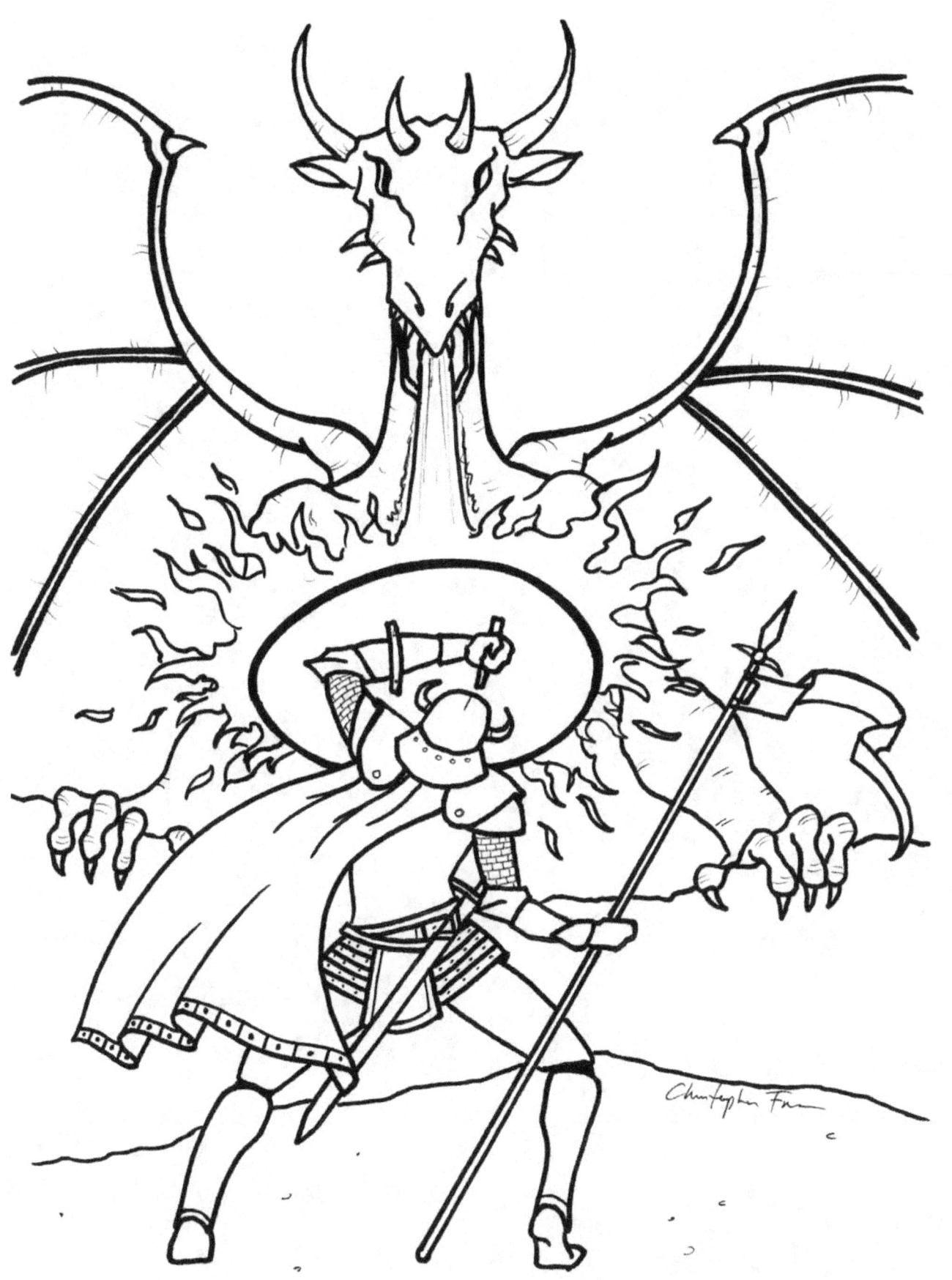

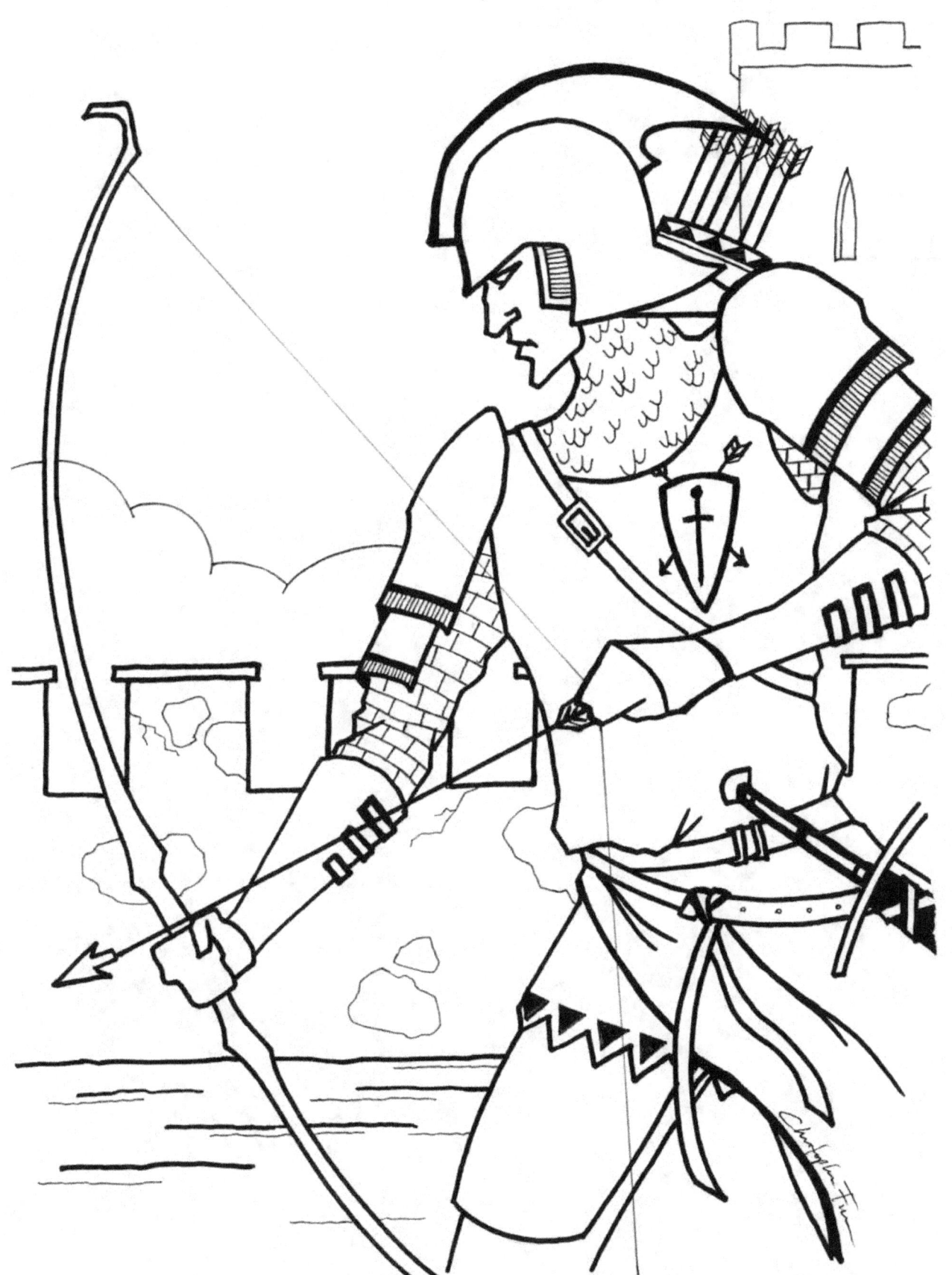

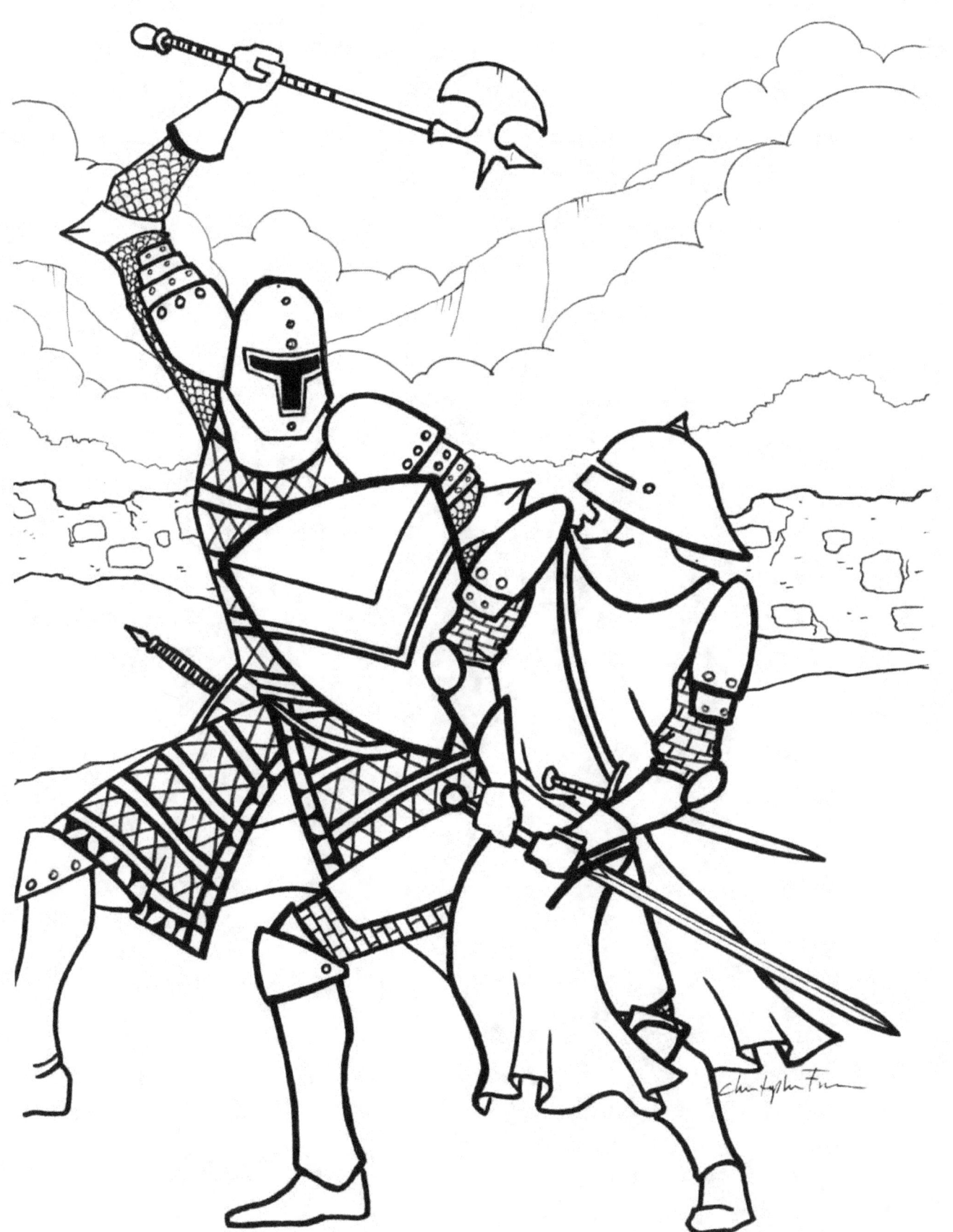

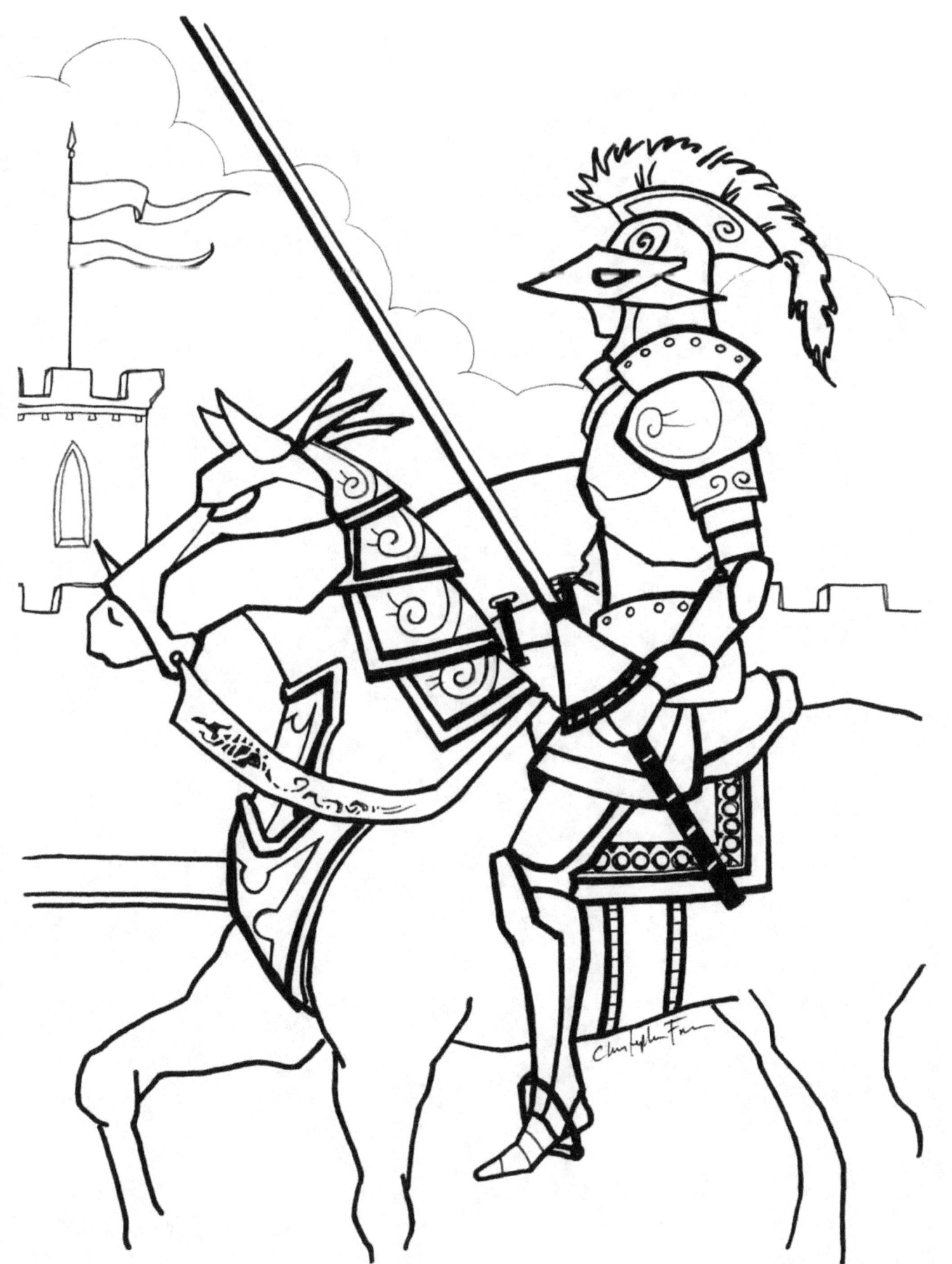

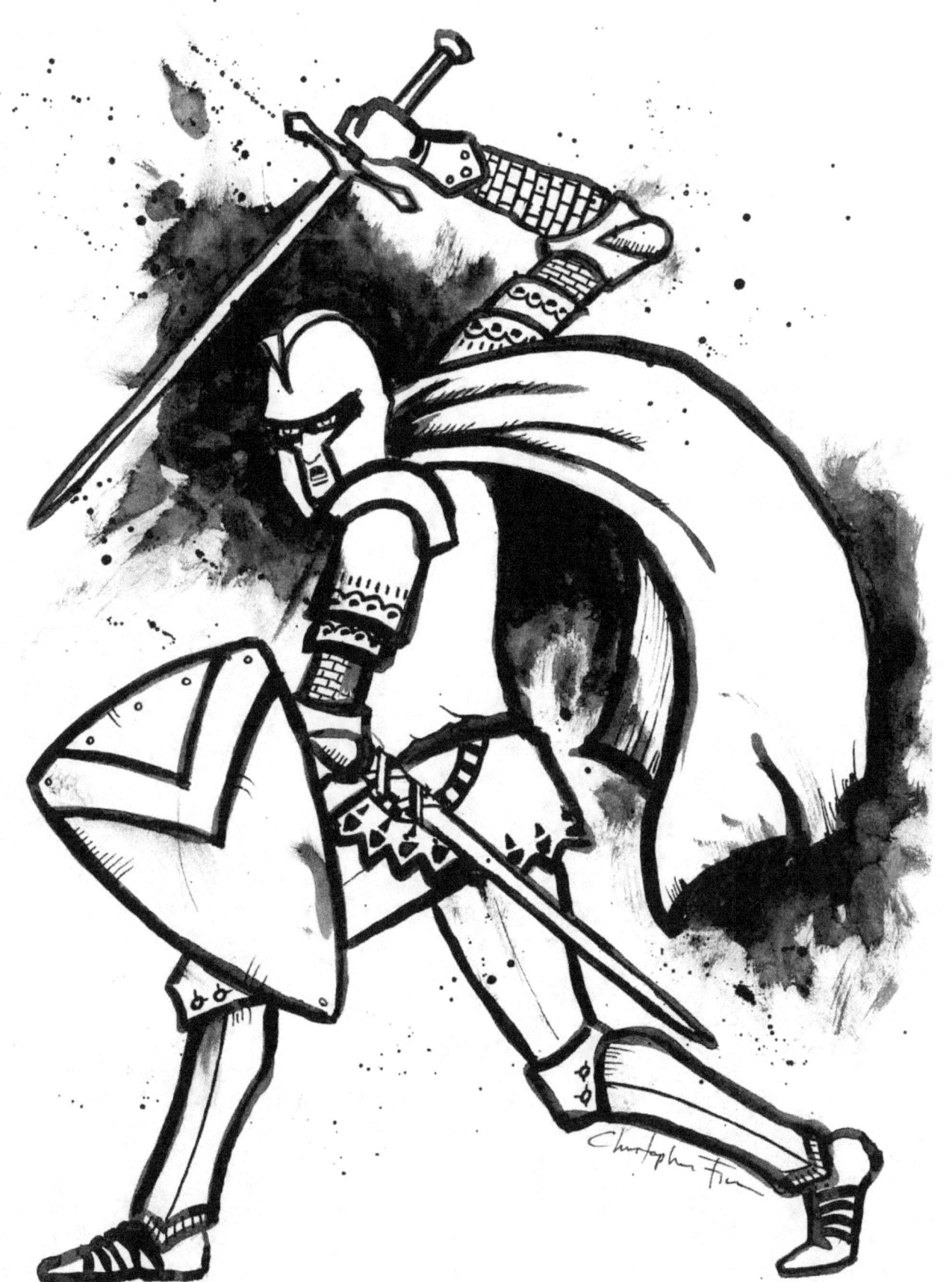

Christopher Finn

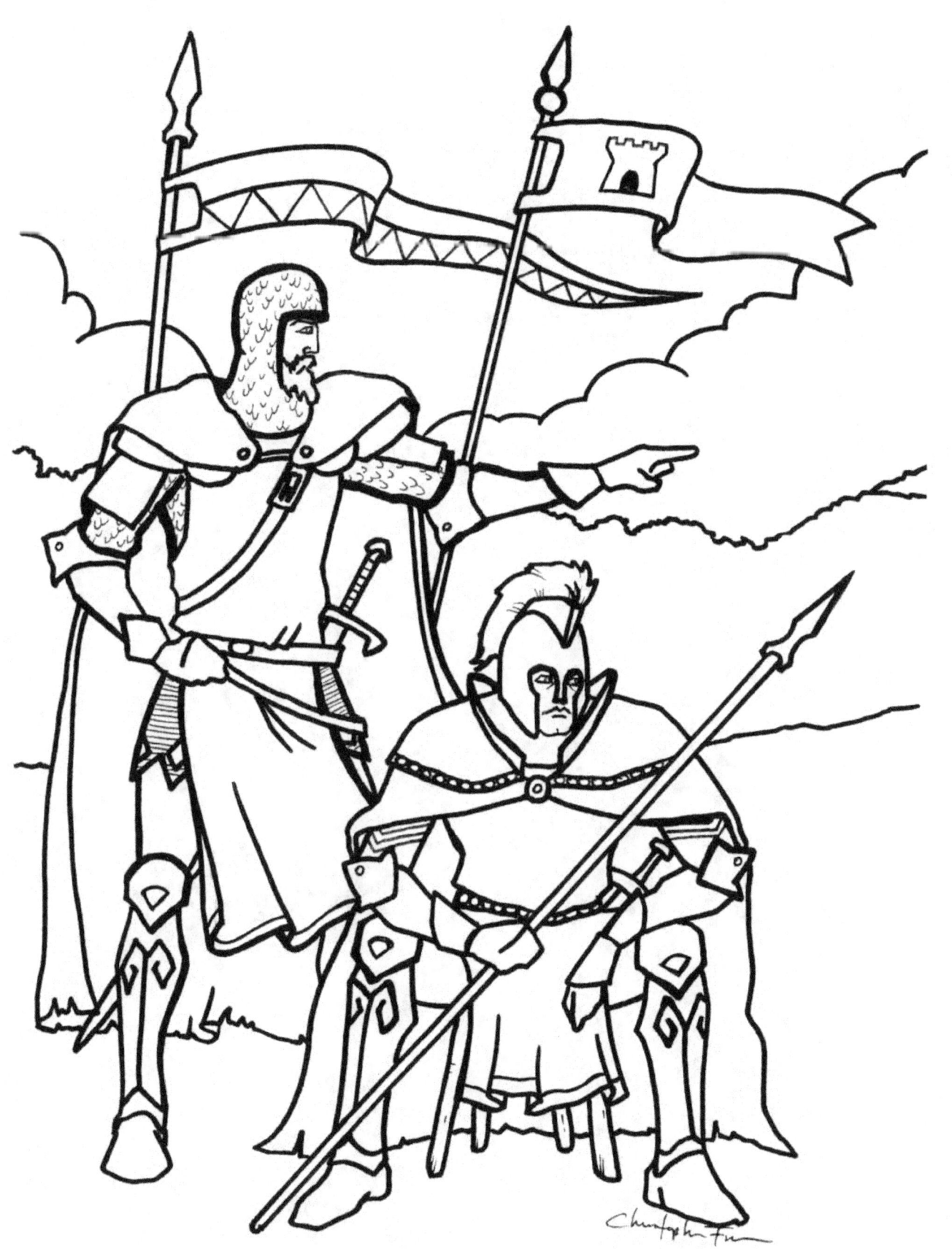

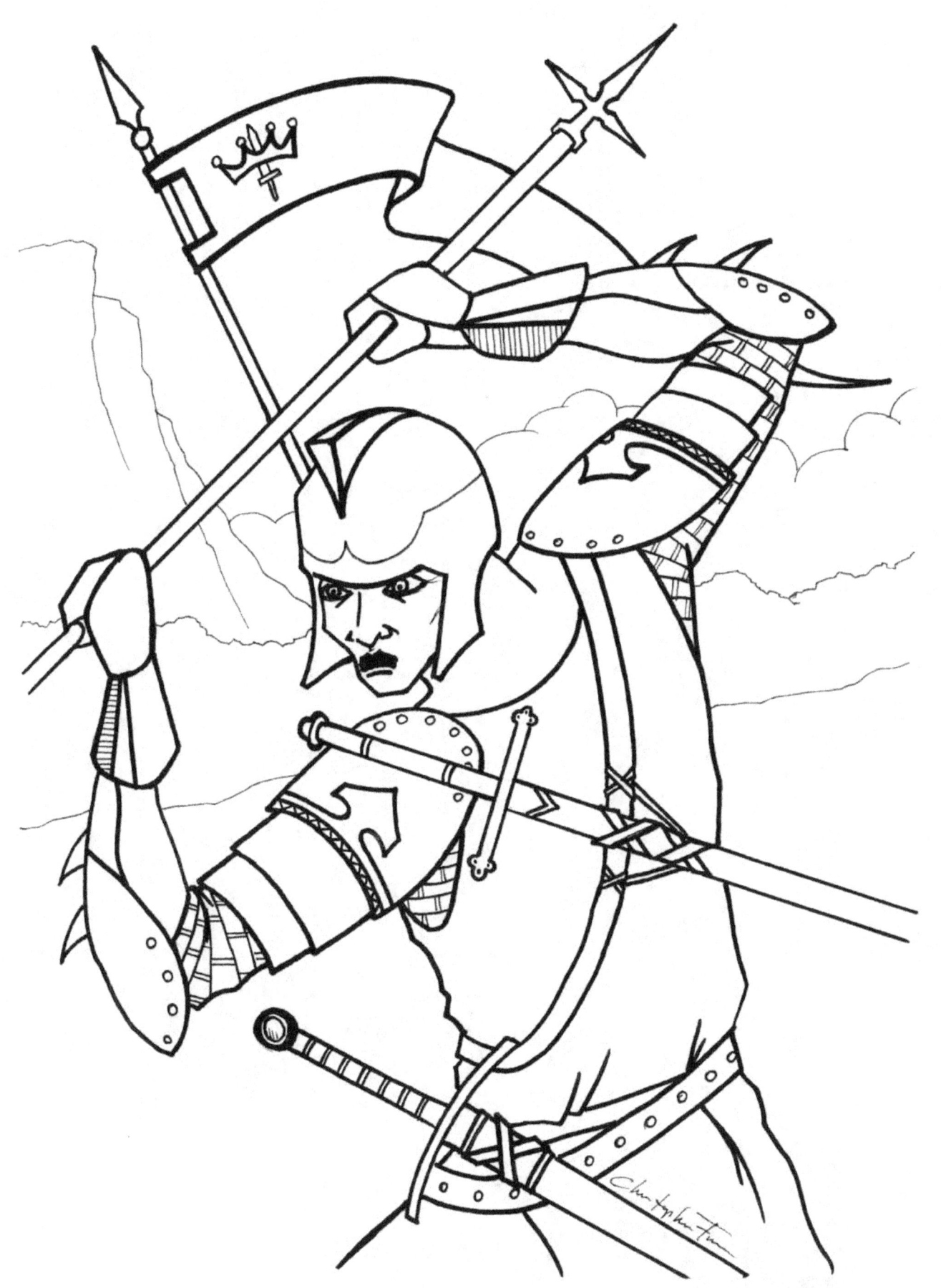

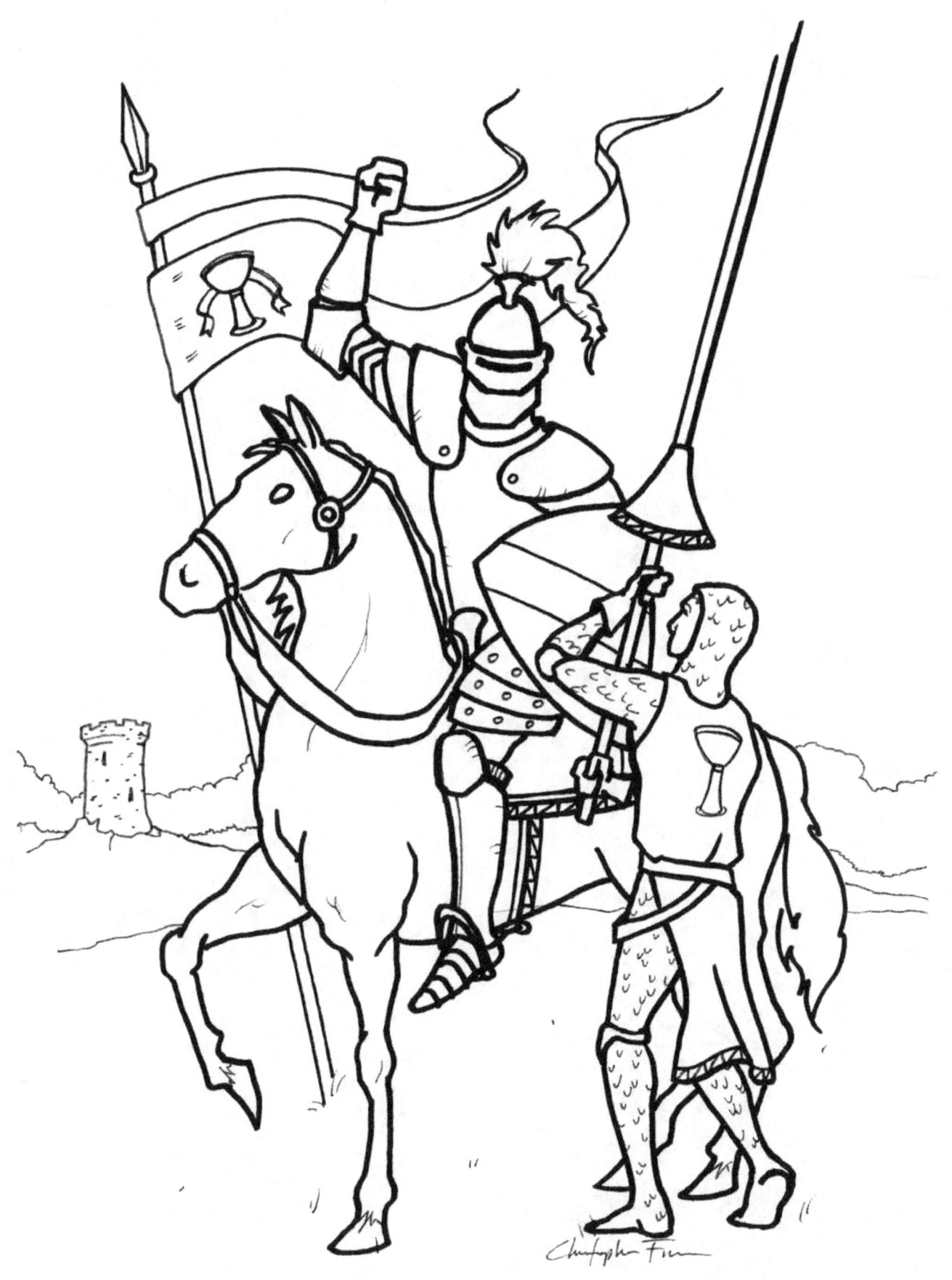

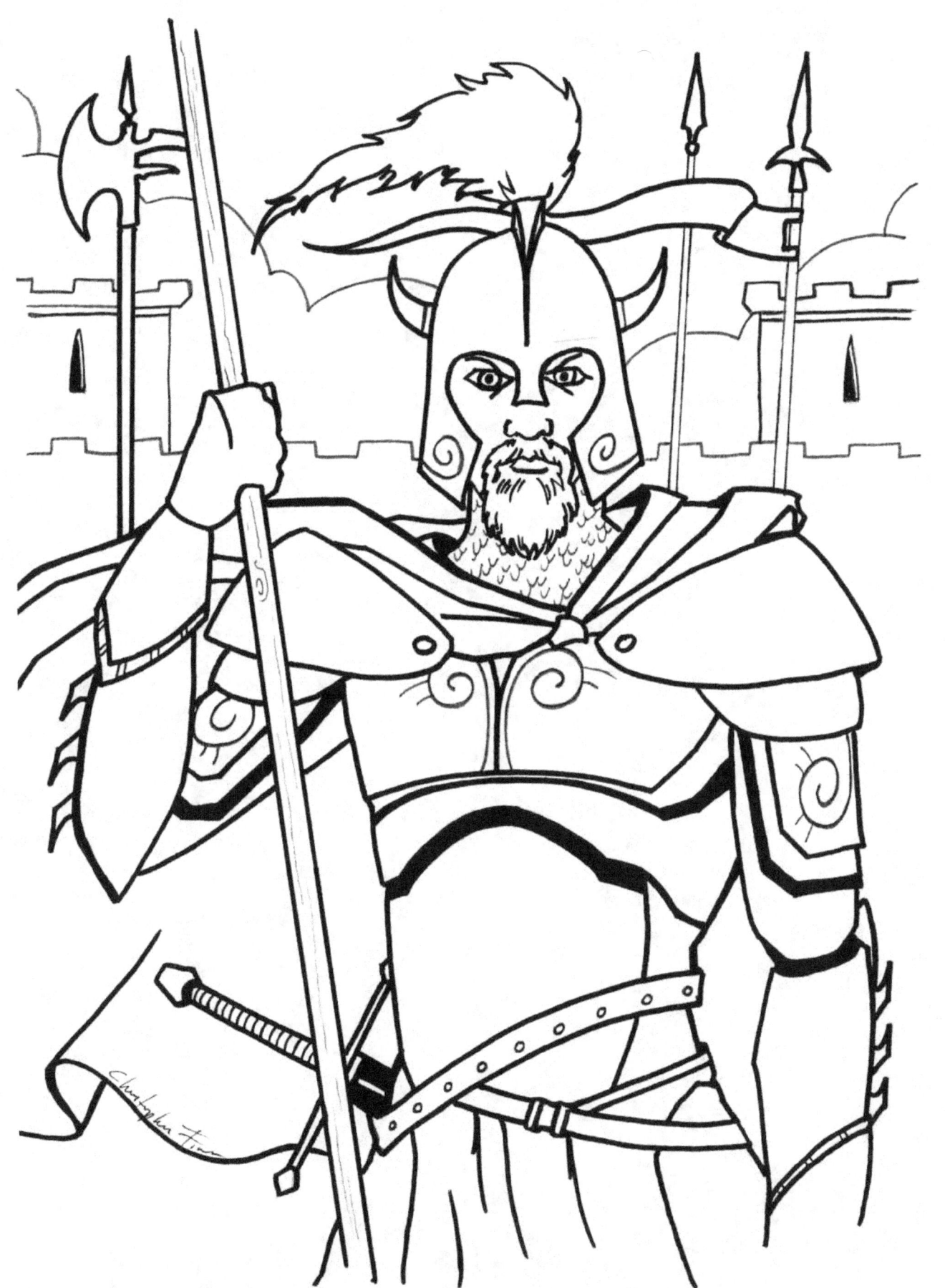

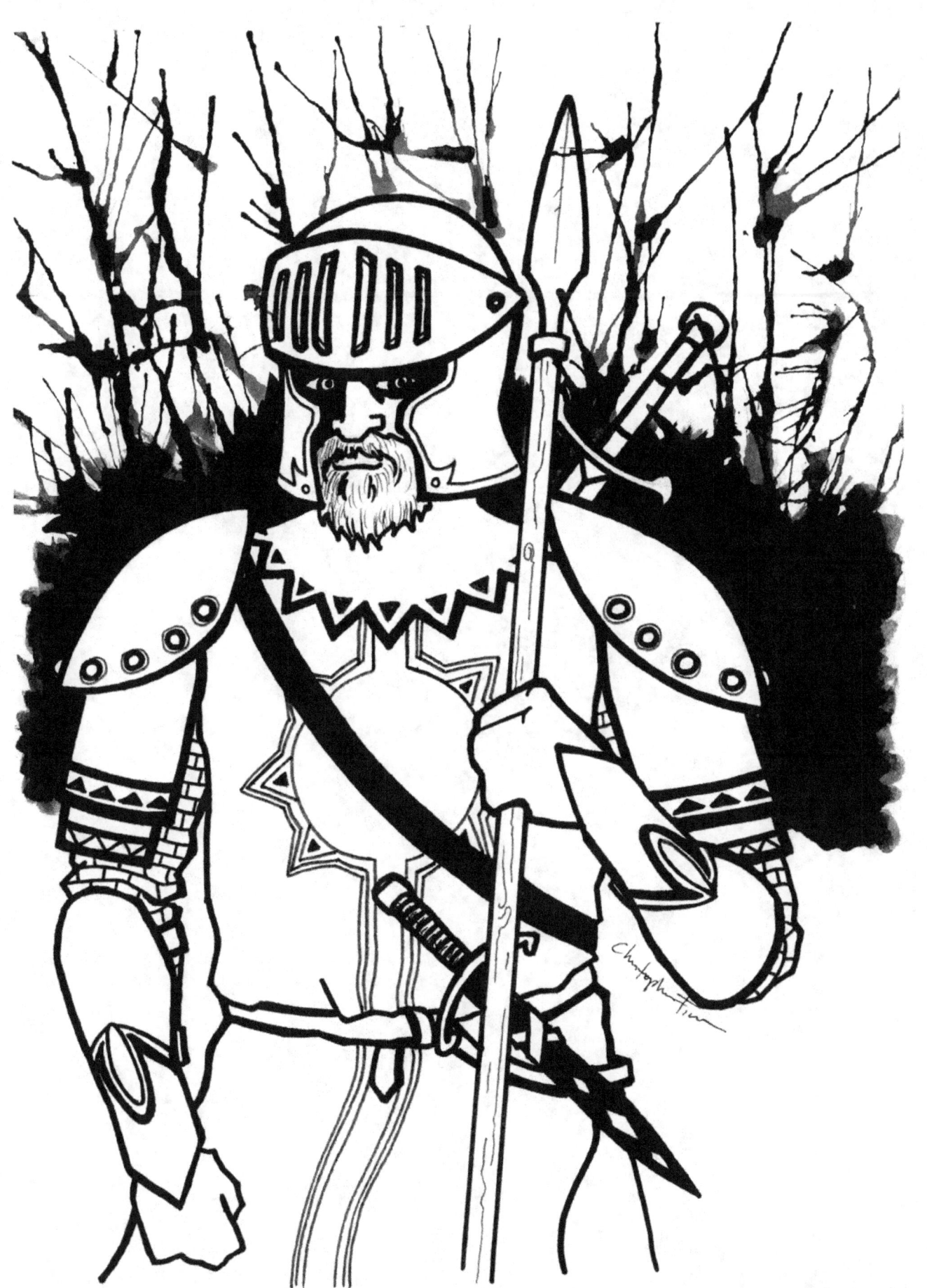

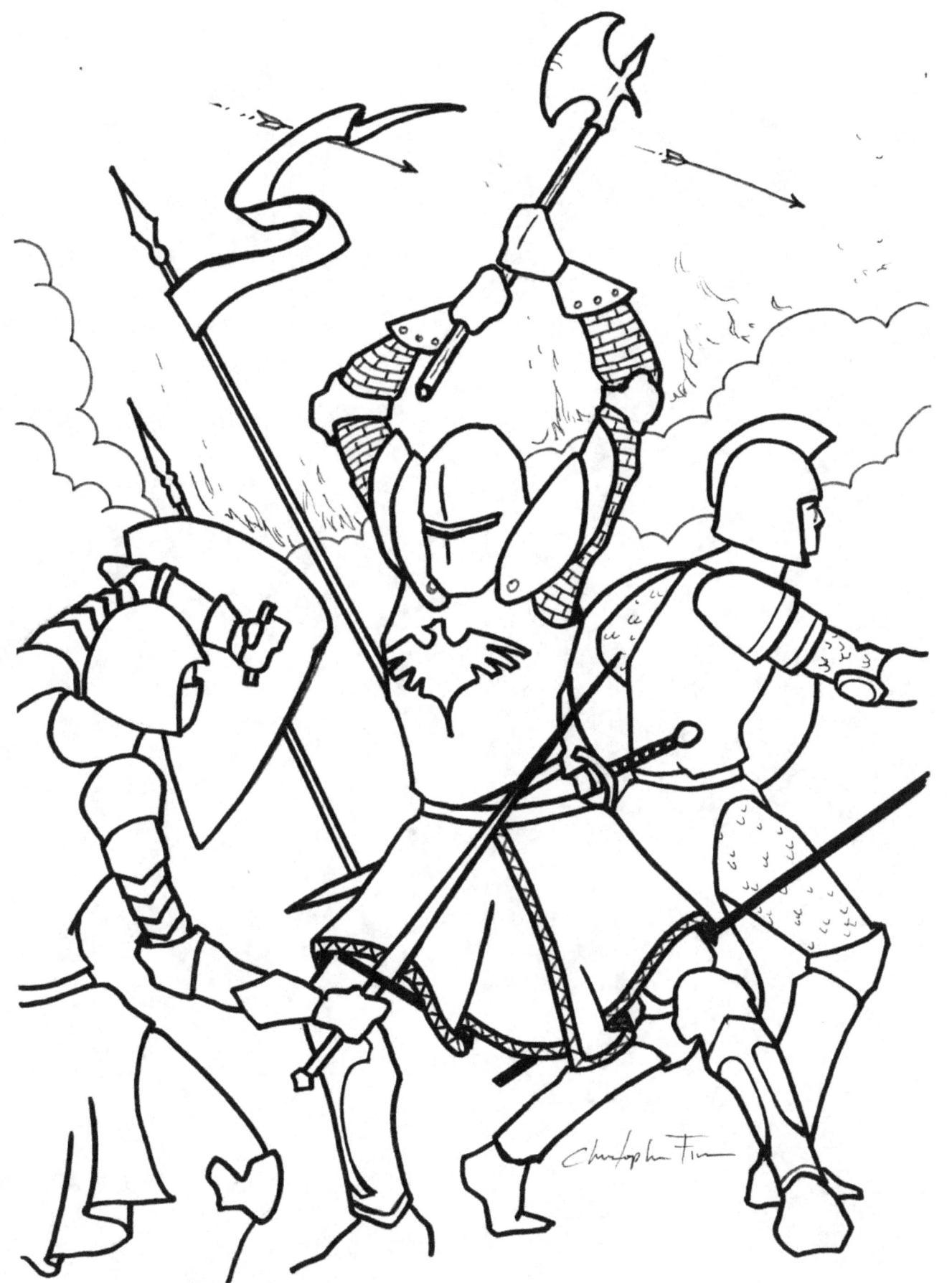

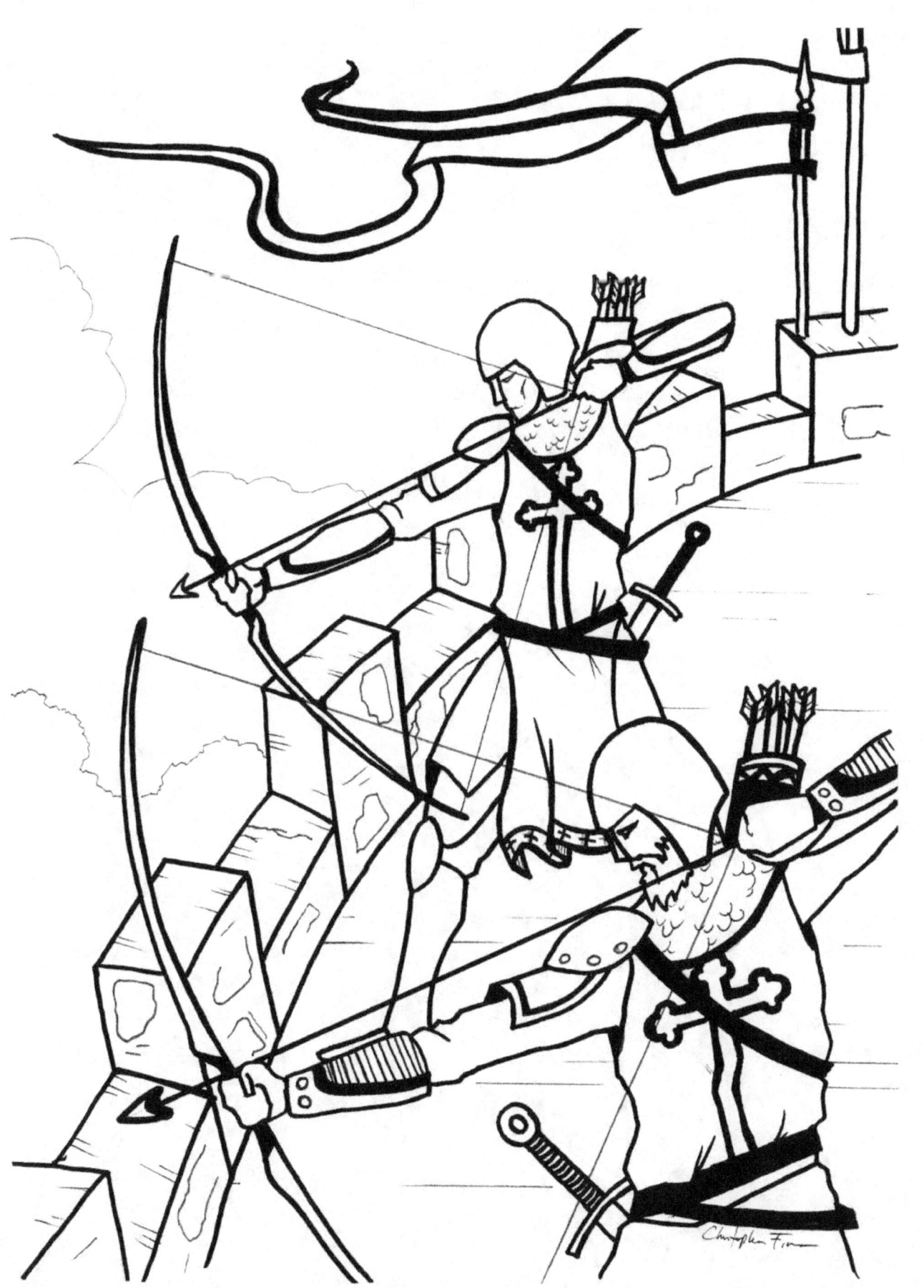

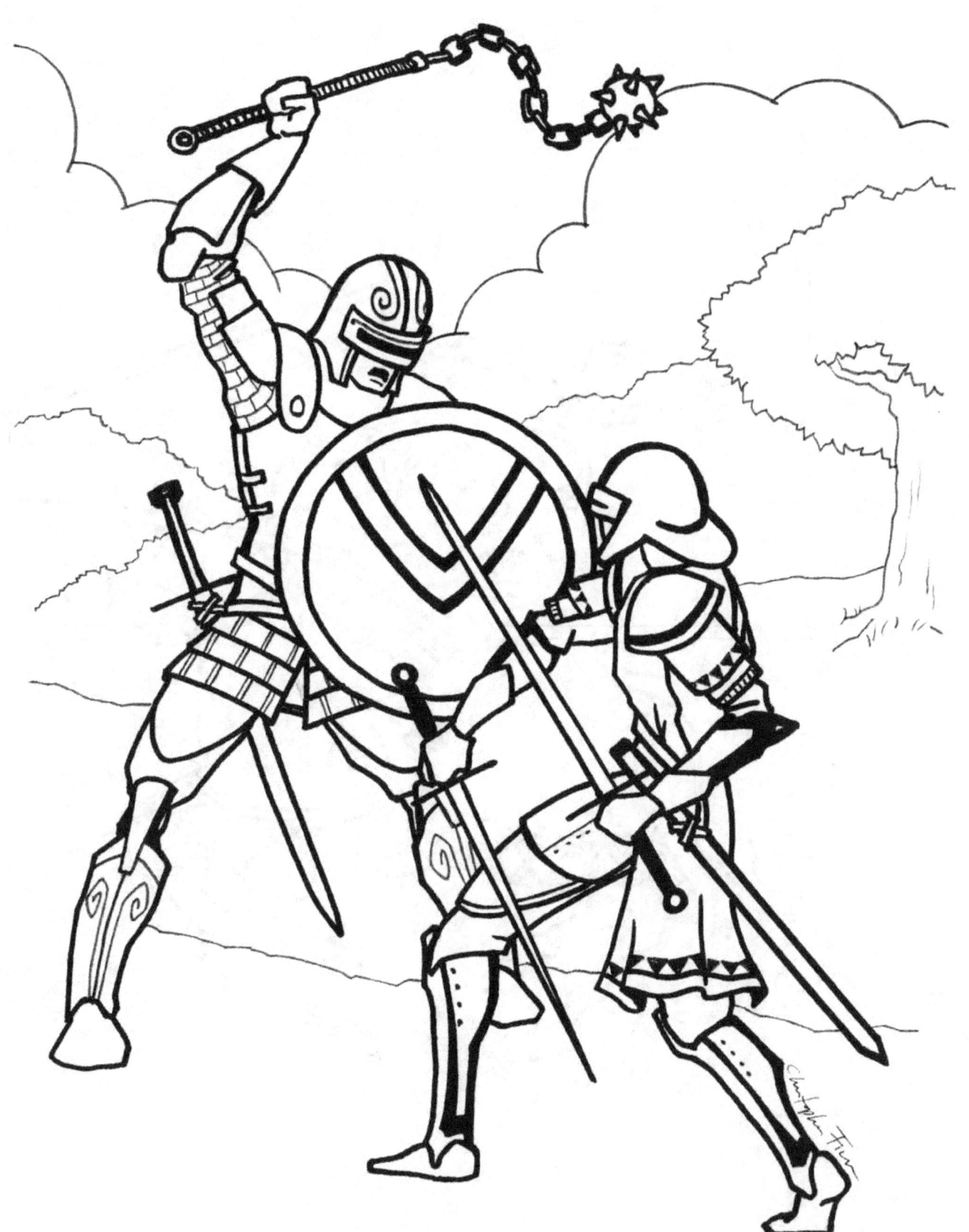

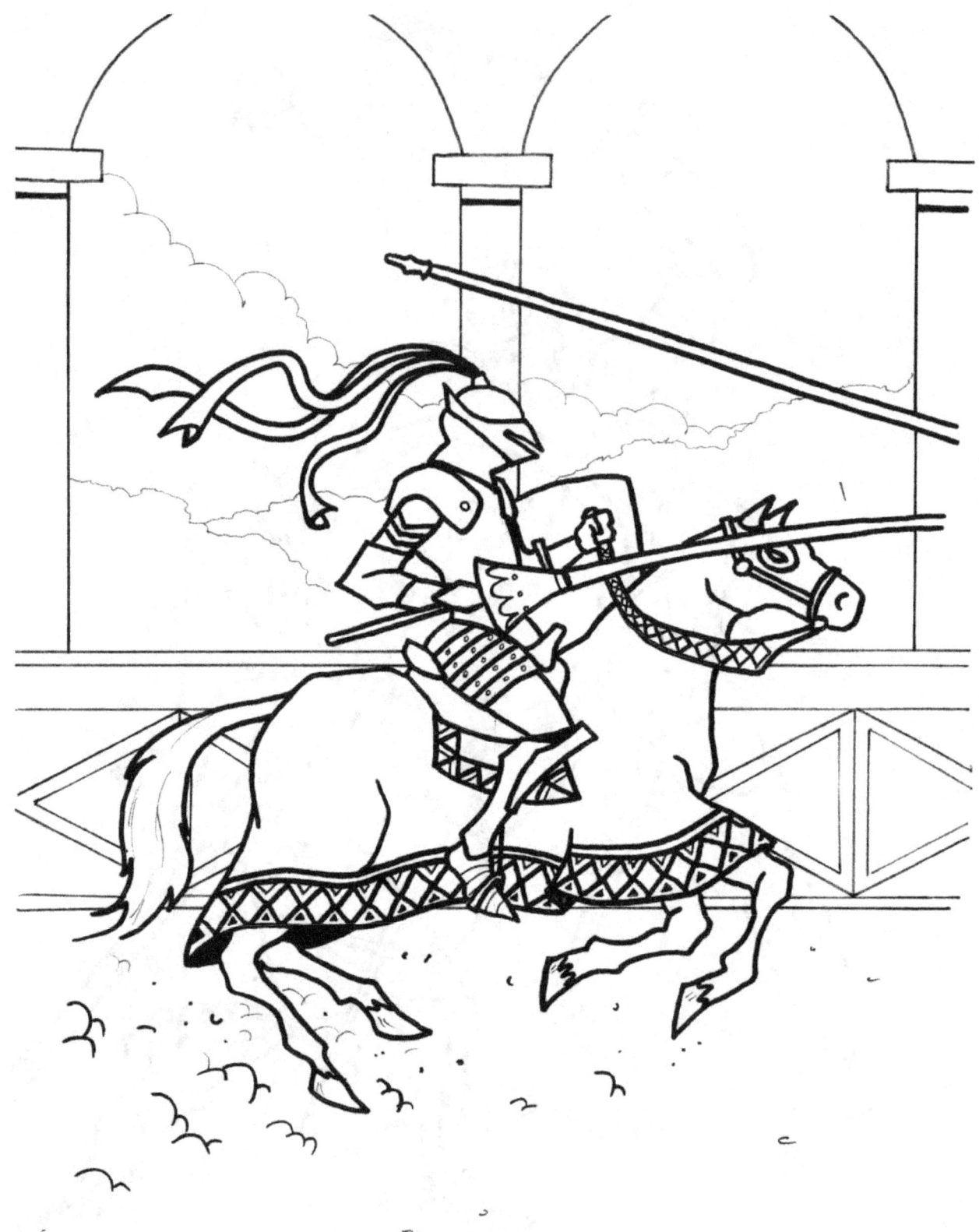

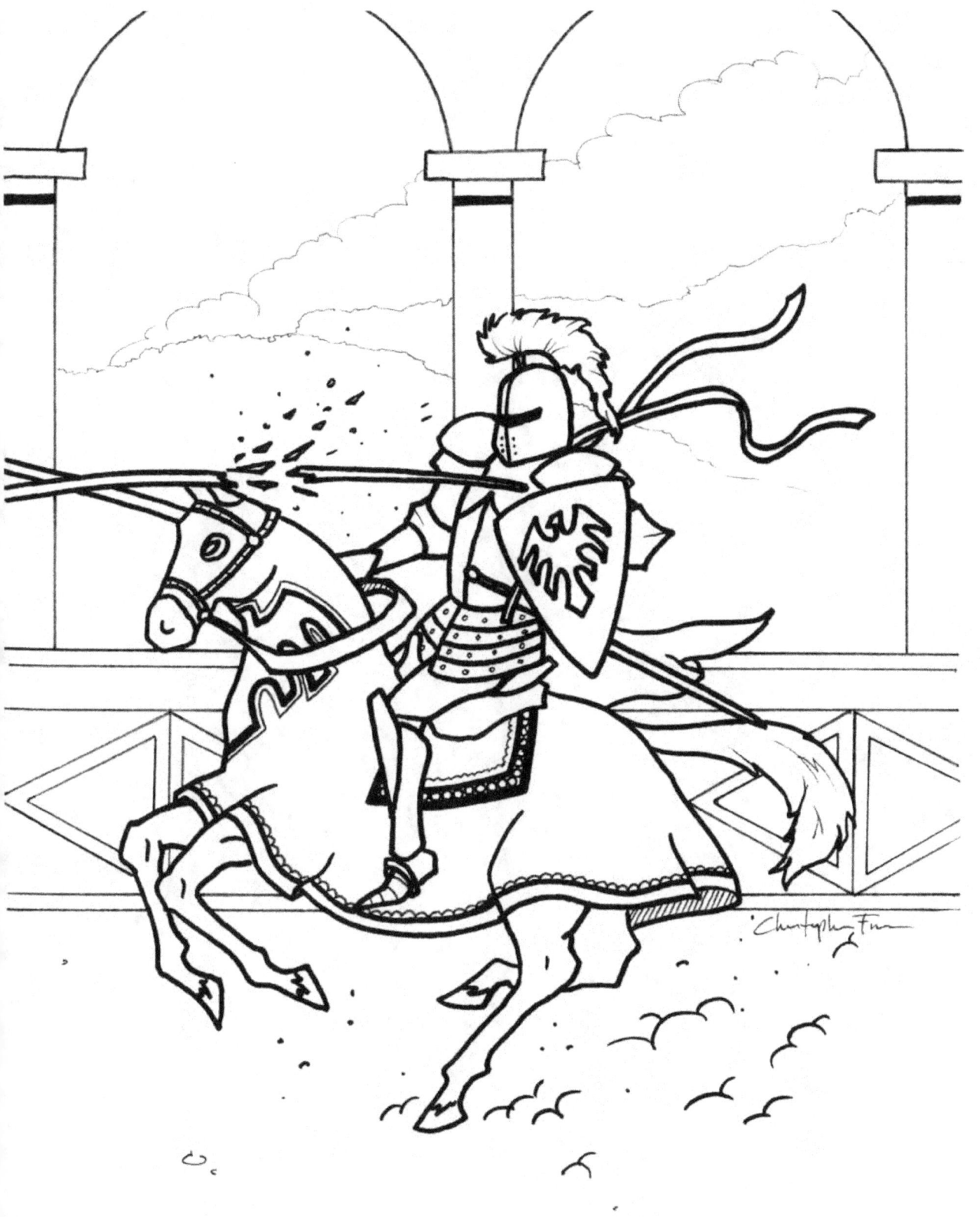

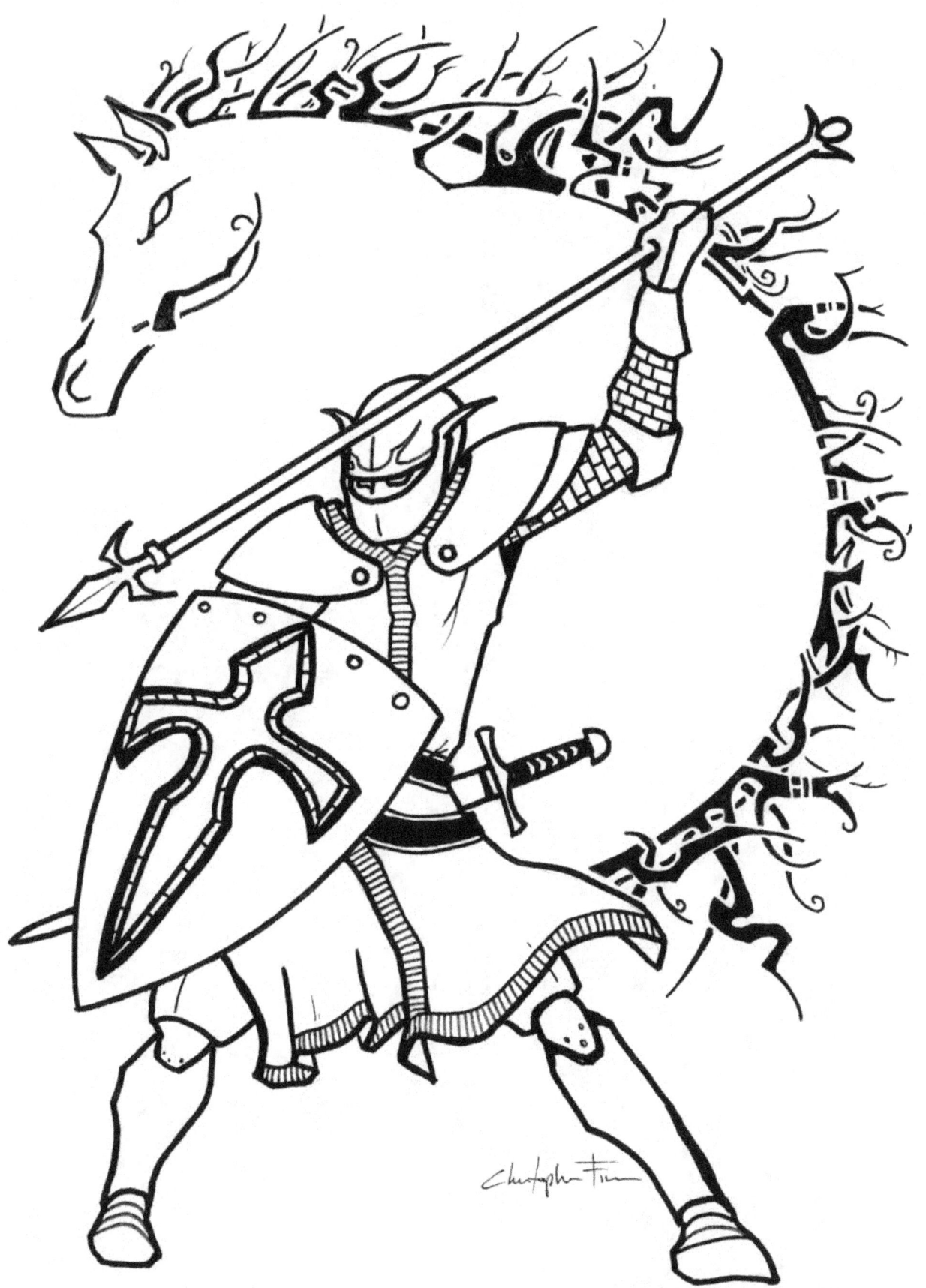

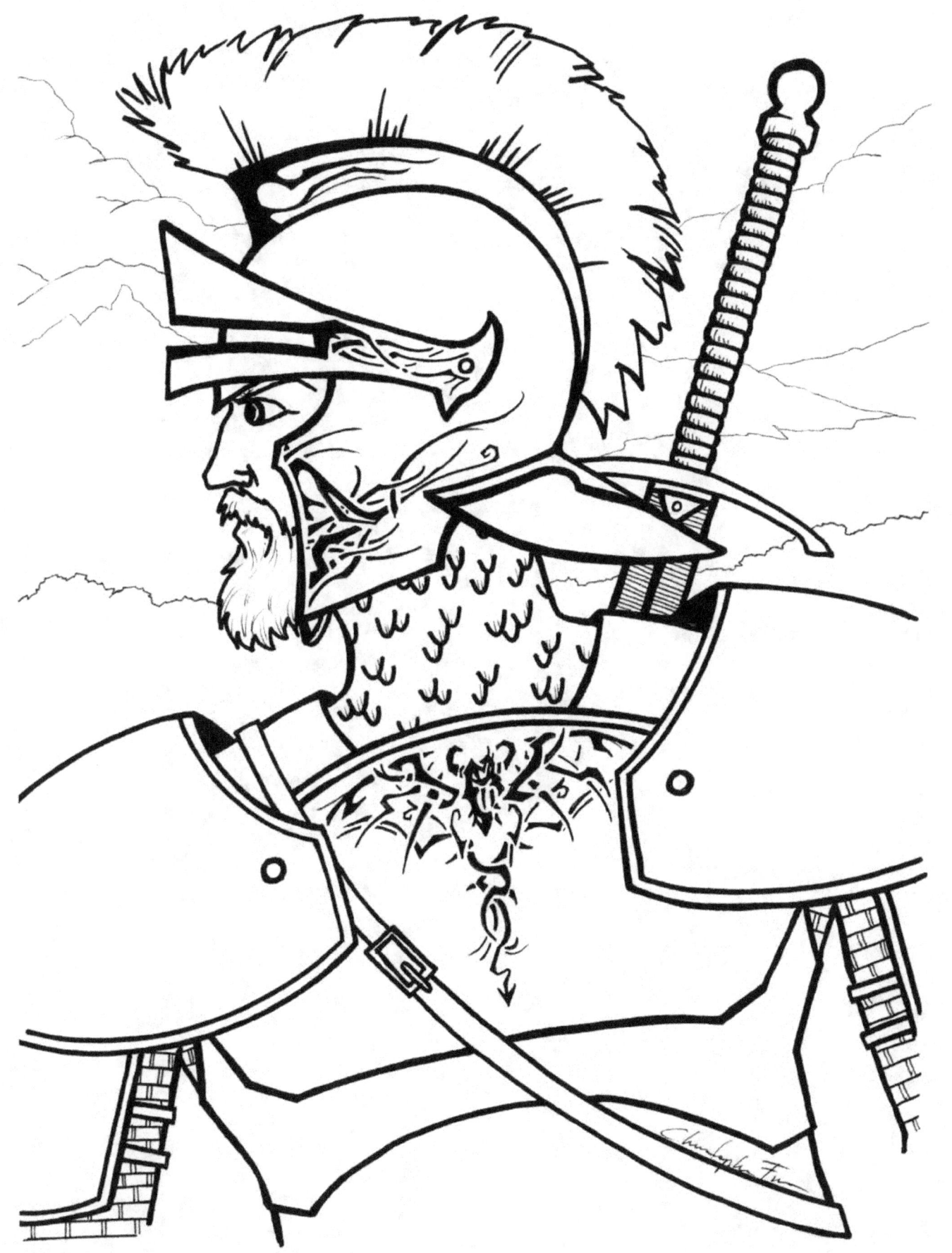

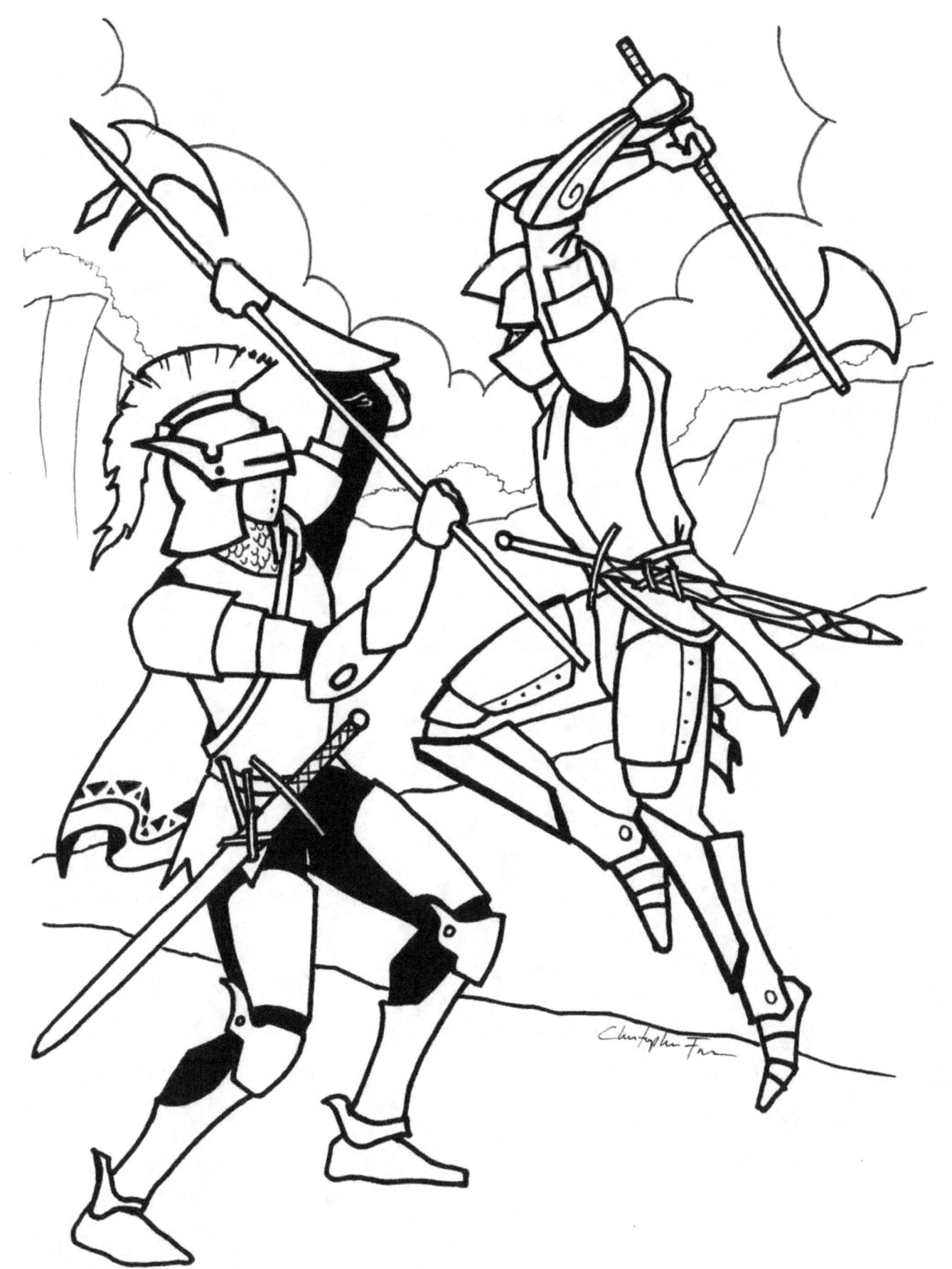

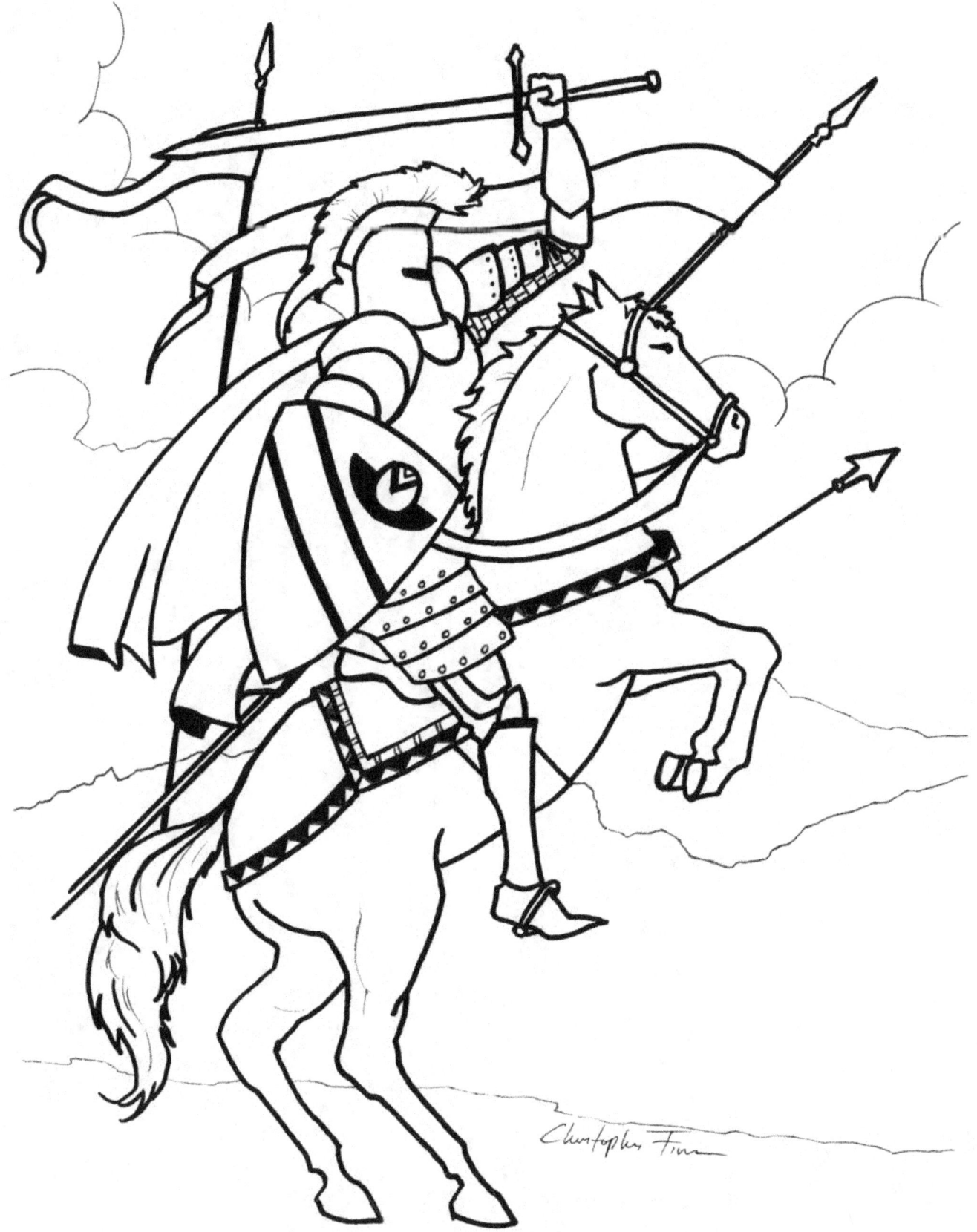

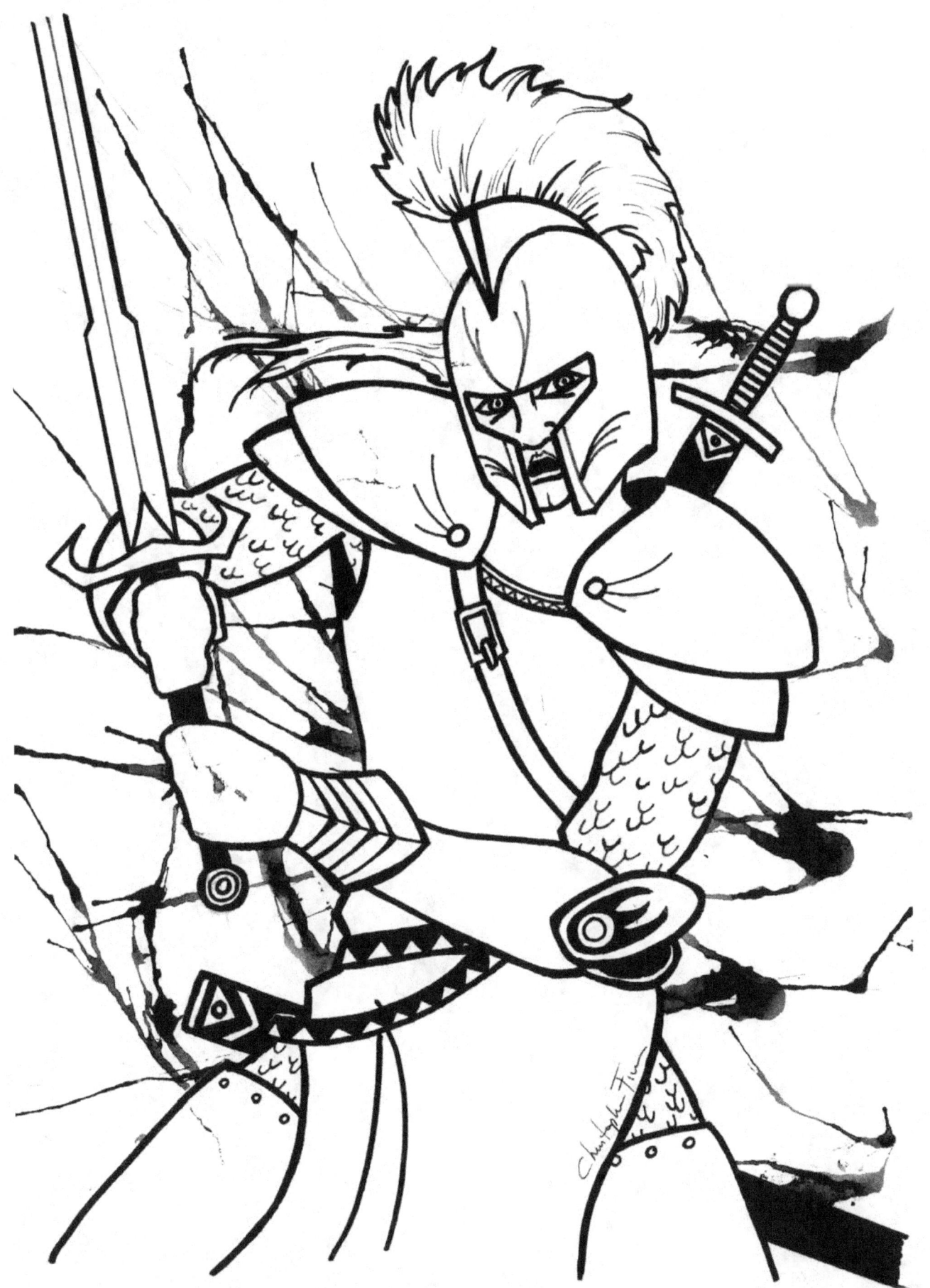

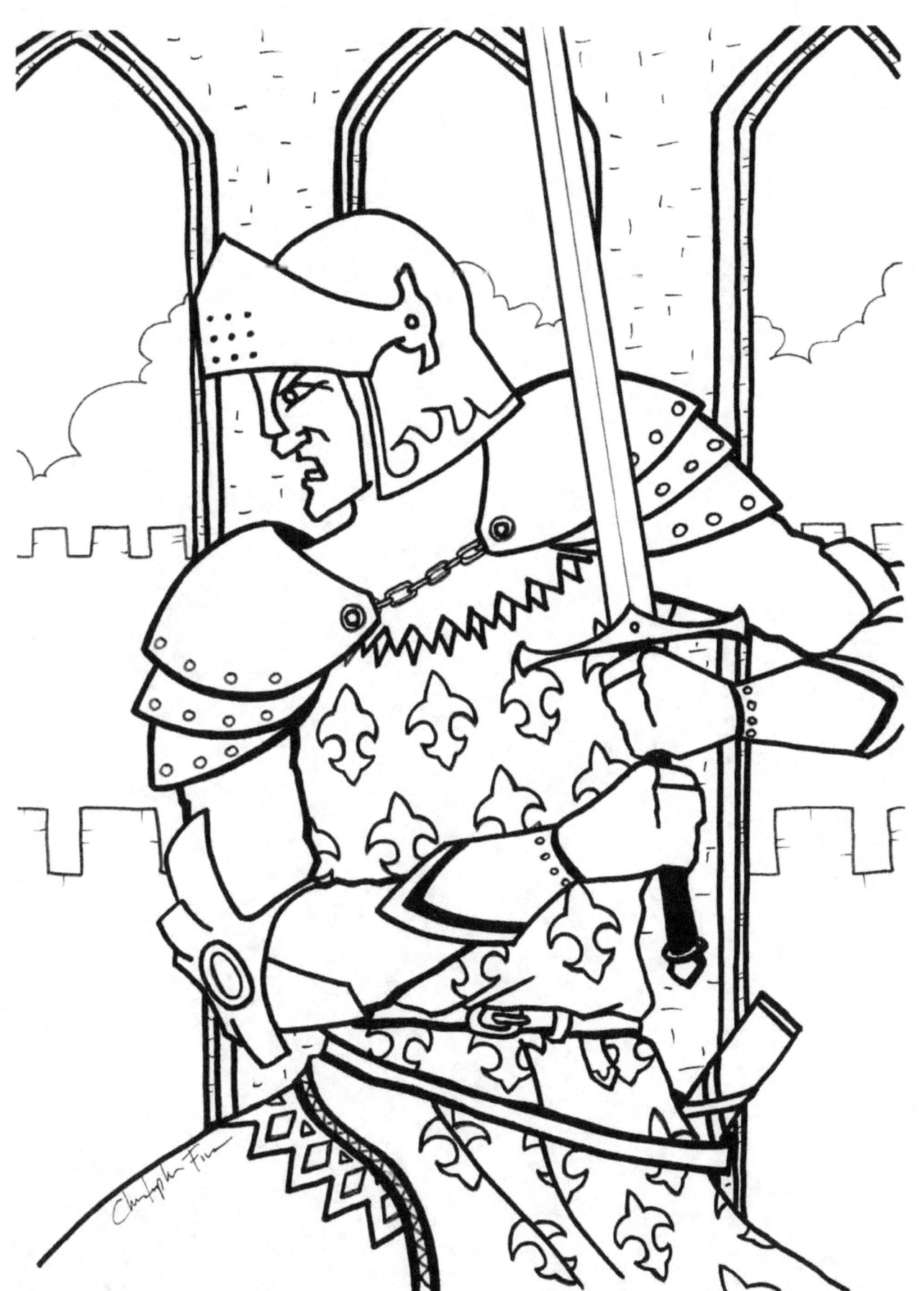

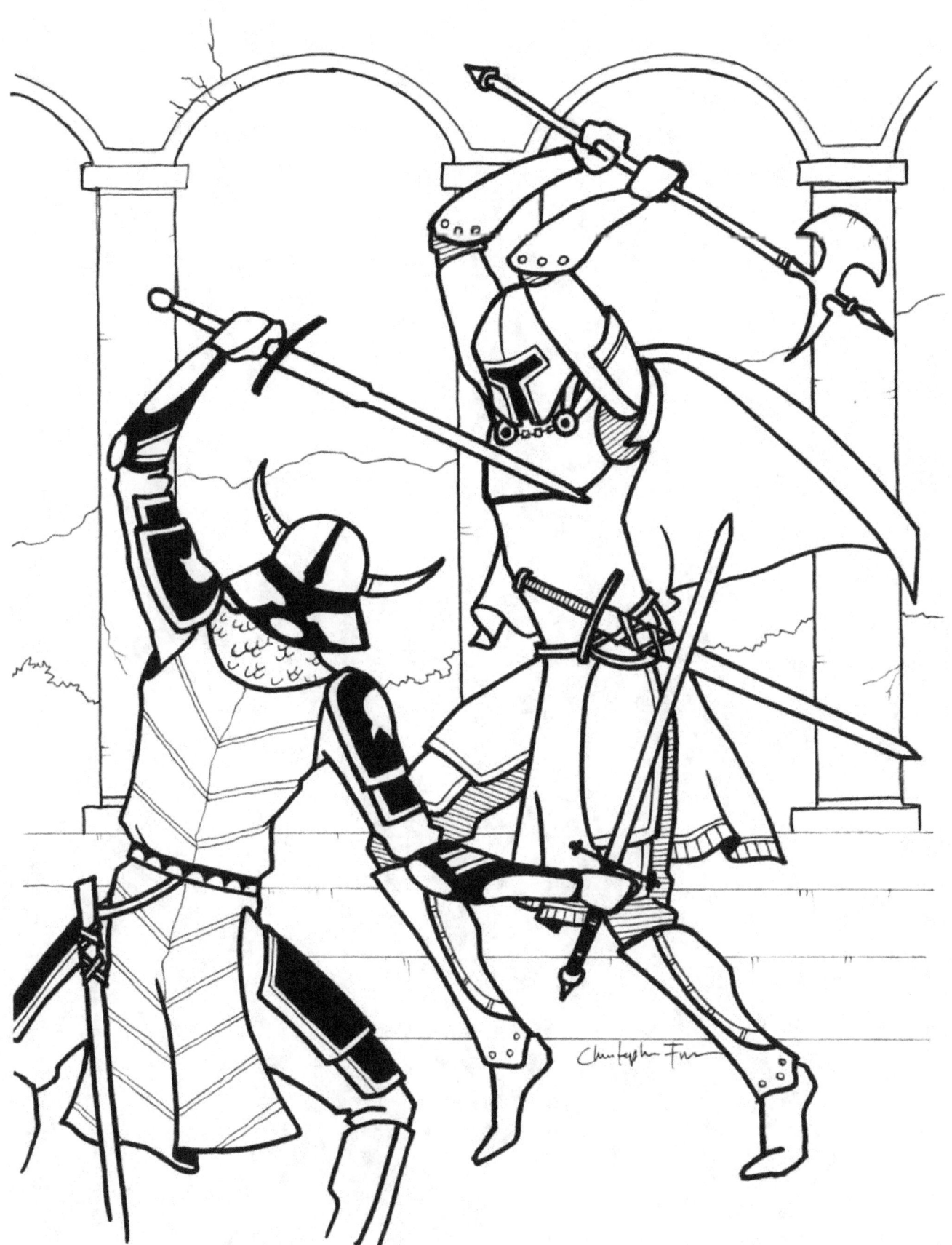

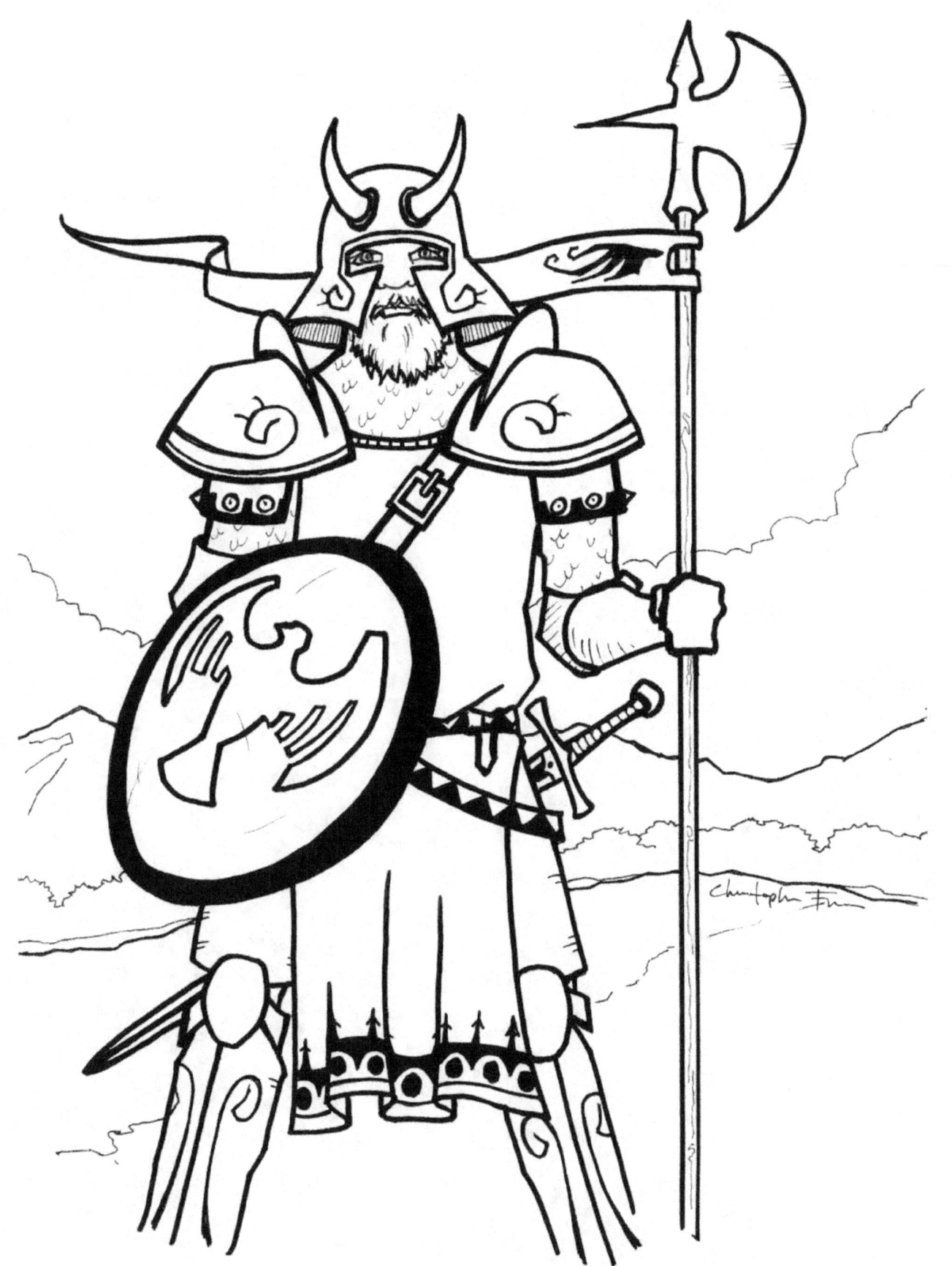

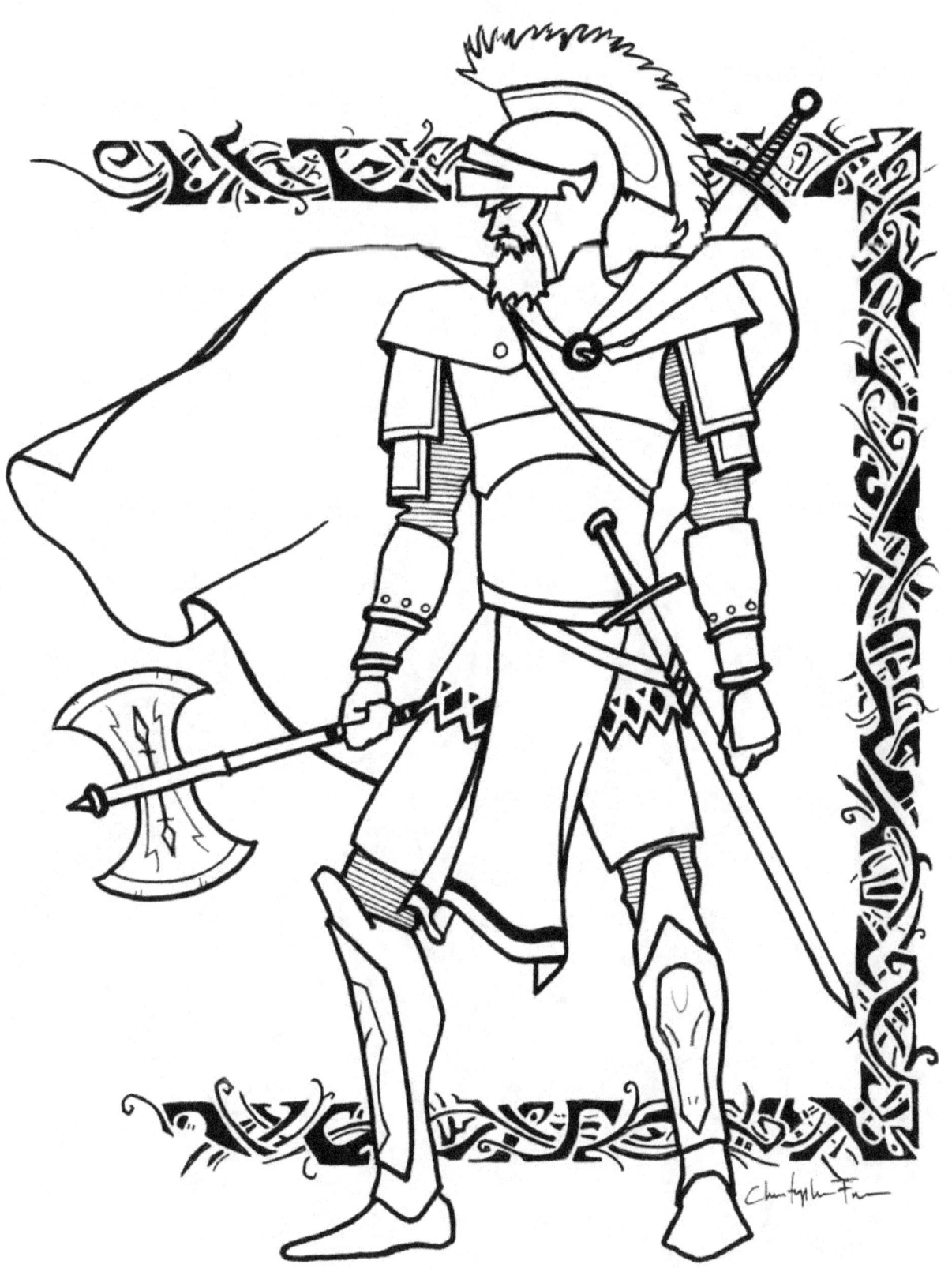

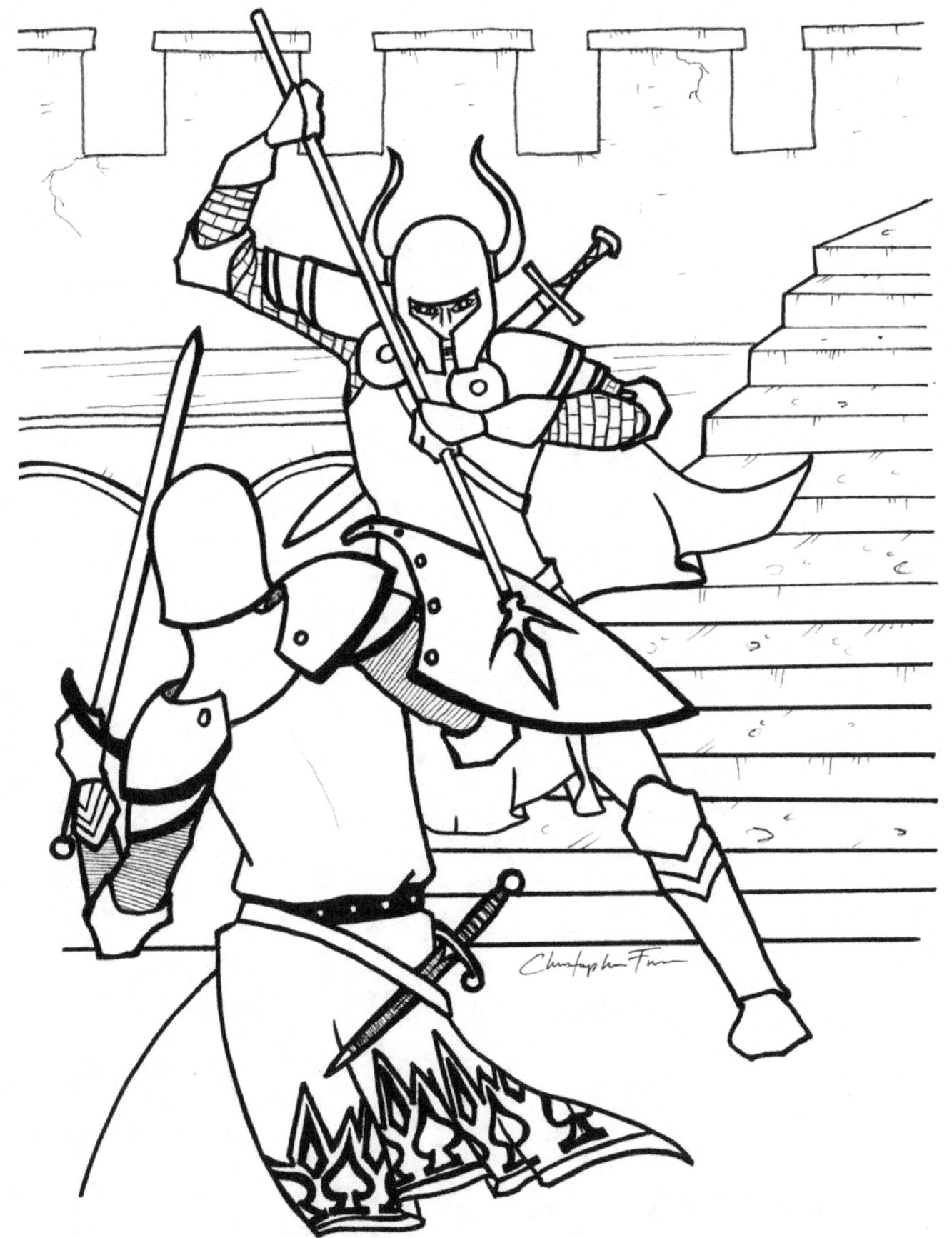

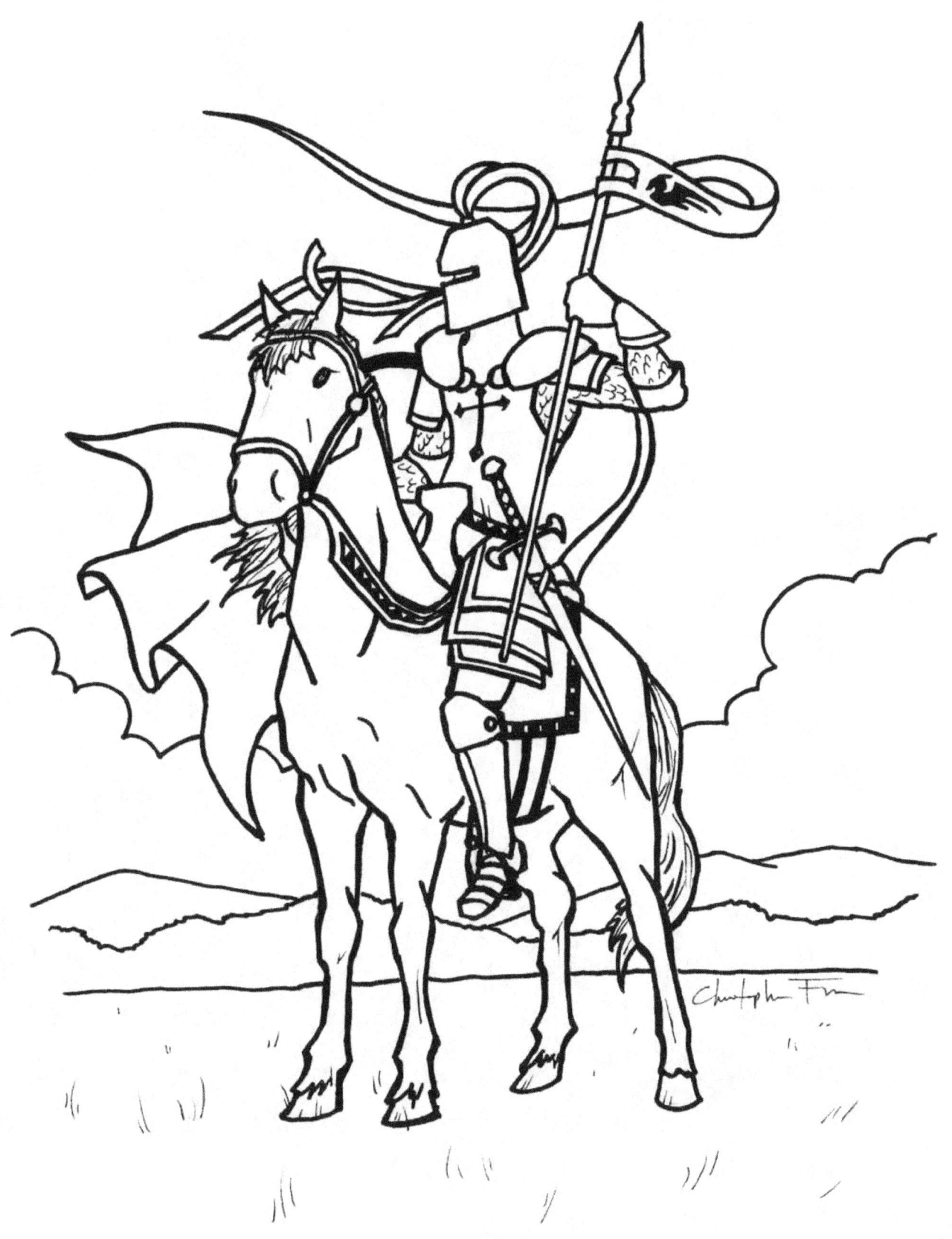

www.ingramcontent.com/pod-product-compliance
Lightning Source LLC
Chambersburg PA
CBHW081216170526
45165CB00009B/2846